W9-BWZ-203

WE NEED
NEW STORIES

WE NEED NEW STORIES

*The Myths That
Subvert Freedom*

Nesrine Malik

W. W. NORTON & COMPANY
Independent Publishers Since 1923

For information about special discounts for bulk purchases, please contact
W. W. Norton Special Sales at specialsales@wwnorton.com or 800-233-4830

Manufacturing by LSC Communications, Harrisonburg
Production manager: Lauren Abbate

ISBN 978-1-324-00729-6

W. W. Norton & Company, Inc., 500 Fifth Avenue, New York, N.Y. 10110
www.wwnorton.com

W. W. Norton & Company Ltd., 15 Carlisle Street, London W1D 3BS

1 2 3 4 5 6 7 8 9 0

Contents

Prologue

When I was a child, my grandmother, a woman from a Sudanese rural uneducated farming family, used to tell me long, elaborate tales about the land and property her late husband owned. She would speak about how large their house was—The Fortress, it was called, because it was the biggest house in the village—and about my grandfather's largesse and business acumen. Her favorite detail, one she repeated often, was how one could not carry a hot drink from one end of the house to the other without it getting cold. While other children were told fairy tales, my sisters and I were fed a diet of wild stories about the difficulties of navigating a large family estate. In addition to the beverage-cooling issues, it seems visitors often lost their way, children had to be on standby at mealtimes to make the long trip to the kitchen for any requests and, allegedly, guests staying in the house could manage not to run into each other for days. If this sounds implausible to you then you would be right. Even as a child, the whole unnavigable fortress business seemed to be, above anything else, a highly impractical arrangement.

Still, I wanted to believe it. When, in my teenage years, I finally visited the seat of the Maliks in northern Sudan, the treasures, the land and The Fortress, the tea-cooling distances were in fact puny, deserted and crumbling. My grandmother, by now deceased and thus unavailable for interrogation, had lied. I obviously knew on some level that she had embellished her tales, but her fantasies were so removed from the reality (the mud dwellings in which I was standing) that I was angry at her but also a little angry at myself. I felt like the deluded greedy treasure hunter, carrying a map with an "X" marking the spot where the birthright jewels are buried, only to find that the rocks in the treasure chest held no precious stones. I was an idiot at the end of a morality tale about pride and gluttony.

It should have been obvious to me that there was no Malik loot. Along with my grandmother, we had two uncles and an aunt squatting in our Khartoum house throughout my childhood. Sometimes when the house was busy, they were forced to sleep in the yard. It was either a nonexistent, or very illiquid treasure. But after a wave of self-loathing at my own eagerness to believe that I was the descendant of some highborn woman, I felt sorry for her. She had lied—but also in a way she hadn't. She had spun and then believed her own inventions because she needed to. Her stature, severely diminished by her husband's untimely death and his poor economic planning, meant that at the age of twenty-five she was an impoverished widow with five children. The stories had to be woven to sustain her, to create a cushion on which to land as her real status plummeted. Throughout my childhood I was fed this ancestral myth that still remains fixed for many of my generation of Maliks. It is a sort of private family madness. The story of the tea growing cold is still told by people who were born years after the original fable was made up. It is a fantasy, but a harmless one.

I grew up in a household and culture swaddled in such myth.

The first, most important foundational story was of a Malik family rooted not just in wealth, but in the honor, grace, and quiet nobility of its women. It took a long time for me to realize that this was a trick. If the women focused on being comely and composed all the time, they would never focus on the fact that they were deeply unhappy and limited in their freedoms. It took even longer for me to recognize all the ways history, society, and family had leveraged this flattering sense of relative superiority to ensure that we, as women, not only did not question subordination, but competed at suffering it with perfect self-composure. The cultural myths that we believed in imbued us with such a sense of exceptionalism that, even as our fortunes declined, we carried on with the same belief in our supremacy. Never trying to understand why we weren't thriving, never even acknowledging that we weren't. Several family members, intent on amassing the wealth they were born to think they were owed, racked up huge sums of debt to fund business enterprises, lived the high life, then were promptly marched to debtors' jail. The myths had made us blind to our faults. Blinded by entitlement, we never questioned ourselves. Even as we gradually succumbed to bankruptcy, eviction, and public humiliation, the family remained pugnacious and scornful of others.

So, I ran away and moved to the UK before the myths consumed what was left of me. I don't think it's hyperbole to say that my departure was akin to leaving a cult. I was punished for my departure with the threat of family excommunication and endured long periods of bullying by aunts and uncles. My mental health took such a knock that I almost gave up and went back. When my resistance to family pressure almost crumbled, a friend intervened and stopped me from taking any more calls from home.

Once I gained a footing in my new home, the initial sense of relief—euphoria, even, as I enjoyed simple, basic freedoms after a life suffocated by narcissism and denial—soon melted away. I had naively built an idealistic image of a West where, sure, things weren't perfect, but where the basics as far as social justice was concerned had been ironed out, or at least where attempts to iron them out were ongoing. I was not prepared for all the ways my new home was different, but also the same as the one I had just left—with a different sort of tribalism, a different manifestation of misogyny, a codified economic system of injustice. The sexism, in particular, was overwhelming as well as pernicious. Here I was again, the idiot with my treasure map. Here were all the myths again, deluding the larger western civilization into thinking everything was fine as it slipped into decline.

Here were all the myths again, telling us that the West in general—and Anglo-Americanism in particular—was special, imbued with some essential virtue, and entitled to success and dominion over others, expecting them as some kind of birthright. I started to write this book in 2017, a year after the election of Donald Trump and the Brexit vote in the UK. Those myths were finally catching up. It was a time of both political awakening and despair, when it was becoming clear that something was not working, where there was fear and distress but also a healthy impulse to resist and mobilize. But the effort was inchoate, and its supporters were still fixated on the idea of returning to a time before it all went wrong, rather than recognizing that things had been going wrong all along. Then the coronavirus epidemic made landfall. The colossal death toll in the US and the UK far outstripped mortality rates across the rest of the world and finally revealed the state of disrepair that Anglo-American political culture had fallen into.

The virus feasted on two countries whose governments had come to power through victories in culture wars, then once in power, let the machineries of state wither. In the grip of the pandemic, the Black Lives Matter protests of 2020 started in Minneapolis and went global. As thousands of Americans died as a result of the botched response from their government, still more thousands marched in the streets to face down tear gas and beatings. The two events are not unrelated. America was failing.

A malignant thread has been running through Anglo-American history, and it is made of myths. These are not myths that animate believers into a shared sense of camaraderie and direction. They are myths that divide and instill a sense of superiority over others. Nations are susceptible to these impulses when going through times of instability, when they become vulnerable to demagoguery, or fall to dictatorship. Again, myths are useful and comforting galvanizers. But when they take hold in democratic, ostensibly affluent societies, it is not a temporary madness, it is a culmination of events.

My focus in this book is on the US, with some supporting examples from the UK. However, I am keen to stress that mythmaking is not confined to these two nations, and to demonstrate that notion with comparisons to my own experience and those of other cultures.

I have chosen what I believe are the six most influential myths behind the culmination of events. Each myth has what I identify as a "tool," an argumentation technique that advances it. These myths are spun by those who get to speak, who have the platforms, those who have historically accumulated the necessary influence and power. Those who, culturally, are defined as its vessels. Myths are spun out of several untruths, woven with skill, and their omnibus weights the narrative in favor of those who are not necessarily in power—it is less calculated than that—but of those who benefit from power.

My hope in this book is to tackle the ways in which history, race, gender, and classical liberal values are being leveraged to halt any disruption of a centuries-old hierarchy that is paying dividends for fewer and fewer people. This is not a "resistance" book. It is not a guide to activism. It is not a reflection on "how democracies die" or how authoritarianism is on the horizon. This book is an exploration of how resistance is futile if we don't question the very context in which it takes place. My motivations come from a personal prejudice. To put it bluntly, I was damned if I was going to spend my youth taking apart the vanities that blinded me to oppression and failure, only to embrace other vanities that did the same elsewhere. I hope you will read me as a sort of witness to the way myths work and join me in my hope that the most pernicious of them can be successfully exposed.

1

The Myth of the Reliable Narrator

I'm sure you believe everything you're saying. But
what I'm saying is that if you believed something different, you wouldn't be sitting where you're sitting.

—*Noam Chomsky, to BBC interviewer*

On the day of the 2016 American presidential election, I called
a New York–based journalist who was covering the campaign
and caught him just as he was about to walk out of his apartment
and onto the streets of the city to soak up the atmosphere.

"Trump is going to get his ass kicked," he said, "and I wanna be
there to see it." I laughed, told him I was jealous, then went to bed.

When I woke up only a few hours later it was still the middle of
the night in London, but it looked very much like Donald Trump
was not in any way getting "his ass kicked." I called the journalist again.

"It's not looking good," he said. I'm sure I heard his voice catch.

What followed was a media-wide crisis of confidence, one that
roiled the liberal establishment in general. The polls, the reporters
on the ground, the holy goddamn *New York Times*' swingometer

all reflected the consensus opinion that Trump was, as my journalist friend had said, going to get his ass kicked. Later the next day, I sat with some other journalists in a London pub. It was a fractious evening. An argument about Hillary Clinton as a flawed candidate broke out. In another tense exchange someone objected to the statement that Trump had a "good instinct." What was really going on among this group of friends and colleagues was that no one knew what was going on.

An almost identical scenario had unfolded a few months earlier. On the night of the EU referendum in the UK, I went to bed after hearing Nigel Farage, the face of the Leave EU campaign, make a pre-concession speech. I woke up to a country that had voted to leave the EU. I plugged news radio into my ears as I left for work because it was all happening so fast. David Cameron resigned as prime minister before I had even caught the bus.

Later that day, the media machine swirled in a vortex—reporters hustled to set up interviews to meet the spike in demand and editors readied new front pages as the industry tried to adjust to the wavelength that it had not picked up. For a few days, it seemed implausible that no one at the top had resigned for their failure to see the change coming. As a columnist, I felt it was surreal to make do with explainers for what happened when I had not written a single piece predicting the outcome. It was the media equivalent of working at a bank on a day the financial market crashed and stock prices went to zero. The industry was caught packaging ideas and repackaging them to the extent that they became completely disconnected from any authentic reporting. This was our own version of subprime mortgages. When the real world came knocking, the ideas were worthless, and no one knew or remembered how the process had worked in the first place. An editor in the US told me that the atmosphere in his newsroom felt as if there had been an assassination. The same applied to my British colleagues. The mood was funereal. How could we carry on as normal? What was the media for? Two paths could be taken at this moment—either we could reckon with all the ways the media is not separate from power in the representative makeup of its body and its independence of thought, or we could deny that there was a problem.

We took the denial route. There was no wholesale appraisal of our failure to report and explain the facts, as opposed to echoing back industry and political class conventional wisdom. Whenever the media fails epically on a moral or reporting scale, whether it is the Iraq War or the failure to take Donald Trump seriously, a few mea culpas are issued but, all in all, nothing changes. This is the norm. Plagiarism and falsification are red lines, but gullibility and lapses in moral judgment are par for the course. If a politician is disgraced, she resigns. If a fund manager loses money, she loses her job. But in journalism there is an impunity of tenure. The fact that we did not see it coming meant not that there needed to be serious introspection, but that no one could have *possibly* seen it coming. We were reliable narrators.

I start with this myth—the myth of the reliable narrator—because it underpins all the rest. Unreliable narrators from academia, the publishing world, and from the journalism industry have been a roadblock to addressing structural inequality. They are the main conduits for communicating all the other myths that prop up the establishment and defend it against movements for change. We believe in their neutrality and thus do not question the accounts of the world which they have recounted to us. These unreliable narrators present themselves as free of bias, of identity, of politics. Their moral and political miscalculations are not benign oversights or human error—they are harmful lies. Unreliable narrators dictate the popular accounts of mainstream history, how we talk about identity politics, and they give intellectual cover to our politicians. The role such narrators play in stemming the tide of change is paramount. We need new narrators to clear the path for change.

Narrators of myths use tools, a set of argumentative techniques that are tailored for each myth. Whenever marginalized groups ask for meaningful social transformation, these narrators wield specific tools to divert attention from grievances and discredit movements for equality.

Our allegedly reliable narrators deploy these tools by leveling certain lines of criticism at their targets. These movements are too woke, too politically correct, too radical, too taken with identity politics, too eager to shut down free speech, too vindictive to respect due process, too righteous, too thin-skinned. Closely aligned with power, these narrators make dire moral judgments for which they are rarely punished.

The Iraq War remains a helpful illustration of this coziness with political authority. While some of those politicians who launched and supported military intervention have faced questions about their decisions to go to war, the ecosystem that forced through their warmongering has not come under any scrutiny despite admissions that mistakes were made.

In 2004, the *New York Times* issued a mea culpa, stating that the editors had "found a number of instances of coverage that was not as rigorous as it should have been." They said: "In some cases, information that was controversial then, and seems questionable now, was insufficiently qualified or allowed to stand unchallenged. Looking back, we wish we had been more aggressive in re-examining the claims as new evidence emerged—or failed to emerge." The main problem was that accounts of Iraqi defectors were regurgitated by government officials, the neutrality of which the *New York Times* simply assumed. Consequently, they reprinted officials' claims about weapons of mass destruction without sufficient question.

In the same year, the *Washington Post* issued a similar apology in a three-thousand-word front-page article. The newspaper said that it "did not pay enough attention to voices raising questions about the war." Leonard Downie Jr., the *Post*'s executive editor, said: "We were so focused on trying to figure out what the administration was doing that we were not giving the same play to people who said it wouldn't be a good idea to go to war. . . . Not enough of those stories were put on the front page. That was a mistake on my part. . . . The voices raising questions about the war were the lonely ones. We didn't pay enough attention to the minority."

The *New Republic*, which had broken with the left-wing orthodoxy in supporting the Iraq War, also issued an apology: "We feel regret—but no shame. . . . Our strategic rationale for war has collapsed."

It took some individuals a little bit longer to humble themselves. In 2006, multiple Pulitzer Prize–winner and *New York Times* writer Thomas Friedman, a man who has built a homestead on the wrong side of history, came out to say: "It is now obvious that we are not midwifing democracy in Iraq. We are babysitting a civil war. . . . That means 'staying the course' is pointless, and it's time to start thinking about Plan B—how we might disengage with the least damage possible." Three years earlier, he was calling for France to be voted "Off the Island" (i.e., out of the Security Council) for its impudence in daring to oppose America's war. In 2015, Fareed Zakaria wrote: "I was wrong on Iraq." The same noises came from *Washington Post* columnists David Ignatius and Richard Cohen. Most of these statements came with a caveat that these journalists could not have known better because government spokespeople were assumed to be credible.

In 2013, before ISIS arose from the war swamp to meddle with this neat appraisal, the *Times* of London columnist David Aaronovitch wrote: "Ten years after the war began, the country is more secure and democratic. The alternative was Syria on steroids." The *Observer* writer Nick Cohen, in the same year, also issued a similar doubling down when he wrote: "Ten years on, the case for invading Iraq is still valid." There was a wholesale failure on the part of those media organizations, journalists, and pundits—ostensibly neutral and unaligned with the Bush administration or Tony Blair's government in terms of ideology—to separate themselves from the agenda of power. This rendered them indifferent to the fate of millions of Iraqis. There was a lack of rigor, default gullibility, moral narcissism, and a haste to publish without proper investigation.

Where are most of these people now? Failing upward, for the most part. Friedman is still at the *New York Times* and continues to write the kinds of articles that betray a fondness for power at the expense of the truth. In 2018, a few months before the Saudi regime assassinated the journalist Jamal Khashoggi in its Istanbul consulate, Friedman spent some time with the Saudi crown prince, returning to write a paean on the modernizing leader who was directing his own country's "Arab Spring" from "the top down." Fareed Zakaria was boosted up from his position as a *New York Times* columnist, and went on to become the anchor on an eponymous CNN global affairs show; Aaronovitch and Cohen still have their columns.

Judith Miller, the main *New York Times* journalist on the WMD beat, was not disciplined even after the 2004 apology.

I reach back to the Iraq War generation of liberal journalists and their subsequent thriving to widen the lens on a media scene that, even when forced into moments of self-reflection, rarely follows through into action. What has never really been reckoned with, whether it is war, Brexit, or Donald Trump's election, is the media's role in reproducing the very myths that, when they finally took shape, bewildered its own members.

The main problem is homogeneity. Politically, the opinion-making class is overwhelmingly center, right of center, or right-wing. Demographically, it is overwhelmingly white, male, and upper class. The result is a worldview that is ideologically establishmentarian, unlikely to question government sources, and overly respectful of the offices of power. Received wisdom runs the show. On such received wisdom the *Guardian* columnist Gary Younge wrote: "The political class imparted as much to the media class, and the media class duly printed and broadcast it. The political class, drawn for the most part from the same social class as their media counterparts, then took those articles and bulletins and presented them as evidence. The wisdom was distributed to all who mattered. Those who did not receive it did not, by definition, matter. Within this fetid ecosystem the air was too stale for new ideas to grow." Instead of speaking truth to power, the media class speaks power's truth.

In 2009, the year I started freelancing for the *Guardian* news-paper, a report warned that journalism in the UK had "become one of the most exclusive middle-class professions of the 21st century." It has only worsened since. When I first started writing, it quickly became clear that there was absolutely no path for me, a non-white immigrant with no networks in the media—to become a writer and columnist. The years of low-paid freelance hours I would have had to put in to build the name and a canon of work that would eventually have earned me a decent salary meant that I would have needed seri-ous subsidy. I had to abandon my writing hopes, as did many others my age who entered the precarious world of freelance journalism in the hope of securing a reasonably paid, full-time media job. Those who survived only made it through sponsorship from parents or partners. I had to take a long loop back to journalism. In order to build some sort of runway, I had to synthetically create a trust fund and make peace with the fact that if I wanted a writing career, I had to delay it and take a full-time job that paid me enough to save the money required to see me through the first years of freelancing. I went into finance, reluctantly. But the job enabled me to write in the evenings and weekends, and it funded those all-important first few years of unpredictable, less-than-minimum-wage work. The major-ity of journalists and writers who started freelancing at the same time as me and who stayed in the game by virtue of family wealth had indeed finally made it to secure well-paying roles by the time I was ready to start writing again for a living. I circled the journalism industry for years trying to find a way in, but the pay made that impossible. At the end of every year I spent in finance, I counted my savings and calculated that they would still not be sufficient to cush-ion the blow of a possible five years of journalism gigs on low pay. I finally made enough, but it took me ten years. If I had known it was going to be a decade before I could start writing, I would have abandoned my journalism aspirations without a second thought. While I was trying to figure out a way to break into journalism full-time and not starve, every editor I asked for counsel gave me the same advice—don't give up your day job.

Things in the United States are no different. Research in 2016 by the American Society of News Editors found that women and people of color still made up a small fraction of American newsrooms. An NPR report on the study warned of the danger of this, concluding that "a typical white, male-centric newsroom, means critical stories will continue to go unreported and news analysis will remain unbalanced."

Coverage of Donald Trump's election campaign and his presidency was a clear example of this newsroom imbalance. As race and immigration became themes, important decisions about how to cover the issues, the maligning of vulnerable minorities, were made by news organizations that employed few of those Trump attacked; even fewer of them worked at the editorial helm. Euphemisms and hesitation around the theme of racism obscured the danger and, indeed, the intention of Donald Trump to rule via racial division. The same goes for the coverage of crime and social welfare.

Even after a decade in the industry, I am still shocked by how exclusive journalism is. Finance is an industry that has a bad reputation for being elitist, a notion which I swallowed whole without really questioning where it came from. My finance colleagues were all well educated and had started to make money from a young age, so on the face of it, yes, the industry did look pretty exclusive. But when I moved to journalism, I was shocked by how inclusive my finance life was in comparison. I had swapped a diverse work environment in terms of class, race, and academic background for a world that was overwhelmingly white, male, and almost exclusively educated at private schools. My final job in finance before starting a journalism career involved working with people from so many immigrant backgrounds that the office kitchen was packed with items from all our various countries of origin. The food and drink were usually cheap and poor quality, an echo of deprived or rural upbringings. I had a big can of powdered milk that I could only get on Amazon or from hole-in-the-wall Arab shops in London. I grew up on the stuff, which was vastly inferior to fresh milk but tasted like home. Other tastes of home included cheap Indomie or Maggi noodles, assorted chili sauces, and jars of spices lovingly prepared and sealed by doting mothers all over the world.

Finance is also an industry that has a reputation for being poorly regulated and above the law. On the whole, this is true of the most senior employees. But in my experience, in the sober sector of private equity, there was little margin for error and the culture of accountability was robust. Another shock when I started in journalism was that there seemed to be little oversight from senior editors, or no fear of punishment for a job poorly done. I have yet to know anyone fired for a journalistic misdemeanor such as fabricating reporting (in some instances, fabrications incurred fines and payment of damages). There is an honor-among-thieves element to it all, a cliquey complicity.

White men of a certain class dominate the media and by extension, the public debate. This cohort does the job of myth narration with the instinct of a state propagandist. The fixation on pedigree, the hermeticism of the opinion-forming class, has created a group of public intellectuals, from journalists to authors, who are only equipped to do one thing—uphold the status quo. What is valued is not intelligence and inquiry, but regurgitation in order to provide reassurance and comfort. This isn't to suggest that whiteness and maleness should disqualify a voice and render it invalid, but rather that the current crop of public voices is not made up of reliable narrators.

I am not suggesting that there is a coordinated cabal and that everyone is complicit, that there are no hardworking, well-intentioned journalists and pundits who try and sometimes succeed in testing their assumptions. Instead, I would argue that that there is a media analog to the patriarchy. The *mediarchy*, if you will allow the crude coinage. In this mediarchy there is groupthink born of uniformity in pedigree and a proximity to power via shared networks and values, which means that instead of reflecting reality, it distorts it, instead of embracing change, it resists it. The mediarchy is set up as a massive lacuna, from which all other faults can be seen except its own.

Impunity expands that lacuna. When journalists face no consequence for failing to do their jobs, when they are too aligned with power, when their backgrounds and networks insulate them from vast swaths of the population, myth reproduction becomes a risk. Representation is the first solution to this monopoly of ignorance. We need fewer white, fewer male, and fewer affluent voices in the institutions that are tasked with reflecting the world back to us. It is easy, in fact it was inevitable, that the media missed the rise of white right-wing terrorism—those who are affected by it, and in fact have been warning about it, are absent from its newsrooms and columns. Is it a surprise that the Brexit vote happened when immigrants, so lacking in positions of reporting and influence in the British media, could be presented as a threat rather than an integrated part of Britain? Is it a surprise that conversations about economic solutions to inequality are dominated by scapegoating of immigrants, rather than an examination of the economic system that created that inequality in the first place?

In 2018, Pew Research Center analysis found that US newsroom employees are more likely to be white and male than the overall US workforce. In the middle of an Islamophobia crisis, there isn't even an estimate of the number of Muslim journalists in US newsrooms. Columnist roles are the most exclusive. In the largest circulating national newspapers, there are zero staff columnists who are Muslim. For myth projection to end, for the necessary change to happen, schemes to foster and integrate those from different backgrounds are vital. But most importantly, what is required is a reappraisal. We need to step back and allow the myth of reliability, of neutrality, of nonalignment with a political and economic elite, to fall away from those voices we vest with authority. These narrators are not only letting down the society they seek to inform, they are letting their own kind down, unable to explain the world in an objective manner, or anticipate how it is changing. They will continue to be blindsided by the rise of populism and the virility of authoritarianism that, as has become clear since 2016, turns on the media first. This is the *boomerang effect* of myths. They are bad for everyone.

The stories of grandeur my grandmother told me seemed harmless, but they were part of a wider narrative of ethnic supremacy that enabled the powerful and rich of her tribe to look down on and discriminate against other ethnicities. The stories I was told about finance by a morally disapproving media heaped attention on an industry that was easy to knock, while the journalism world continued to function like a cartel outside the law. Myths eat their young. They protect a small number of people who push them cynically, and they devour a large number of people who believe in them earnestly.

2

The Myth of a Political Correctness Crisis

Oh, okay. You want to be politically correct.

—*Donald Trump to a reporter who refused to take*
off his mask during the coronavirus pandemic

"Privacy rights threatened," read the headline on the Fox Nation news item. In the corner of the screen was a logo that overlaid gender symbols against the colors of the rainbow. Without even turning the volume up, one could tell that there had been some violation, some transgression into a female space. Sure enough, the trailed horror came. A transgender student had, at a school in Florence, Colorado, harassed female students when admitted to their toilets. What was worse than the breach and assault was that the girls' parents had protested, but the school refused to discipline the student. It was a double-sourced story, corroborated by the *MailOnline*, the largest English-language news site in the world, which had in turn lifted the report from the Christian Broadcasting Network. It was also reported by the *Denver Post* and *National Review* and circulated widely on social media.

The report was false. Not false in the way a game of telephone sometimes takes a kernel of a story and then weaves layers around it. This was an invented incident. According to the *Advocate*, a publication directed at transgender people that interviewed the transgender student's mother, no student had reported any actual harassment. The entire account was based on the complaint of a single parent who was opposed to the fact that the transgender student was using the female facilities. That lone parent attempted to stir up support by appealing to other parents and the school administration. When they were not responsive, in frustration the parent went to the anti-LGBTQ Pacific Justice Institute (PJI), which took the supposed harassment to the media.

The school itself only got wind of the scandal which had been apparently happening on its own premises when the press showed up asking to interview the mother of the transgender student. It was also the first time the mother of the student was alerted to a story that had already sent the press to her daughter's school.

PJI subsequently modified its public position from outrage at the claimed harassment to concern that "the intrusion of a biological male into a restroom for teenage girls is inherently intimidating and harassing." This change suggests a realization that no actual harassment had ever occurred, but by then, of course, the damage had been done.

The fabrication wasn't an isolated incident. Stories like this are now part of the news cycle and are rarely about the issues they appear to report. The Florence fiction looked like a classic tale about a contemporary panic—the ingress of male bodies into female spaces, but it was really about something else altogether. What the headlines were telegraphing was that there was a danger, a threat to our well-being that is posed by the excessive *political correctness* of institutions. For the purposes of this chapter, political correctness, or being "PC", is defined as the attempt (just the attempt) to create a framework of equal treatment, of opportunity, and of respect for all.

There was so much eagerness on the part of the media to run with an uncorroborated report because this line of scaremongering is popular, even if it isn't true. The result is that public frequency is set at a high-pitched cry of horror at a new threat of men slipping into female spaces with ill intent and getting away with it because of political correctness.

According to 2018 research by the nonprofit More in Common, 80 percent of Americans believe that "political correctness is a problem in our country." Among conservatives, that number is 97 percent. One London School of Economics (LSE) United States Centre study finds the perception that politically correct norms have taken hold and deprived people of their freedom is so entrenched that it played a central role in the 2016 election of Donald Trump. According to Nick Adams, the author of *Retaking America: Crushing Political Correctness*, "the American people . . . are sick to death of the choking conformity, the intellectual tyranny that is produced by political correctness." When asked what "intellectual tyranny" they are suffering from, most Americans who believe in the suffocating effect of PC culture can't point to a list of specific events, or even to experiences in their personal life. A twenty-eight-year-old woman who describes herself as a "passive liberal" told the More in Common study, "I have liberal views, but I think political correctness has gone too far, absolutely. We have gotten to a point where everybody is offended by the smallest thing." Other respondents gestured vaguely to the fact that political correctness has created a "protected class" of minority identities and that other "religions, cultures and orientations are sometimes 'pushed down our throats to the point of nausea.'"

The LSE found that in 2016 these nebulous concerns, en masse, brought about a backlash against political correctness that amounted to a "cultural revolt." That cultural revolt was triggered in part by the kind of fabricated moral panics that concern transgender students and restrooms.

As the transgender conversation is dominated with such fabulation, the details of the actual crisis go unreported. Suicide rates for transgender and gender-nonconforming people are multiples higher than the national average. Despite a decline in several other developed countries, the US suicide rate increased by 33 percent between 1999 and 2017. Part of the story of that rise is that by 2015, 40 percent of adult transgender people reported attempting suicide in their lifetime. This figure is nine times the attempted suicide rate of the overall American population. Bullying, harassment, and violence, or threats of violence, were all cited as reasons for this elevated rate. Black transgender women are particularly vulnerable—they made up 91 percent of all transgender or nonconforming murder victims in the US in 2019.

Despite the specter of political correctness stalking the land, hate crimes against minorities in general are also rising. In late 2019, the FBI revealed that attacks motivated by bias or prejudice peaked at a sixteen-year high in 2018. Physical assaults in particular were up, amounting to more than half of hate crimes. This is personal. A country is raging against its minorities, and contrary to any nonsense about political correctness, it is being emboldened to do so. Latinos in particular have suffered the most. Since Donald Trump came into office, and after a strong start stigmatizing Muslims, his focus then shifted to immigration from Latin America as the incipient threat. The crisis of political correctness is a myth.

Like all good and effective myths, the PC crisis looks like it is a response to a current assault on a variety of shibboleths, but in fact it is a rehashing of themes that are decades old. To those panicking about political correctness, any challenge to male, white, and heteronormative power is a subversion of the natural order of things. While researching this chapter, I was astonished to discover how far back the leveraging of political correctness against progressive causes stretched, and how identical the tools of assault were in any given example. It is doubly astonishing that this particular myth was allowed to develop in plain sight. Its objectives were not very well hidden, and we have had years to contend with sleight of hand. Today, the fact that a public can be primed to accept tall tales about political correctness enabling assault on young girls in restrooms while a vulnerable minor is savaged by the media demonstrates both the mainstreaming of the myth and the failure in challenging it.

The best myths are both old and new. They are old in that they have been in practice for a long time, but new in that they have the ability to keep refreshing themselves, adapting for every new era. That political correctness is sacrificing free thought for uniform oversensitivity to gender, race, and sexual orientation is the oldest and most pedigreed of contemporary political myths. This "oversensitivity" entered the PC lexicon in the mid-twentieth century. The purpose of this myth is to undermine efforts for change by presenting them as sabotage, as attacks on a society that is fundamentally good and not in need of reform. In 2002, conservative commentator Roger Kimball identified the problem as college administrators "falling over themselves in their rush to replace the 'white Western' curriculum of traditional humanistic studies with a smorgasbord of courses designed to appeal to various ethnic and radical sensitivities." Now the myth has renewed itself into relevance once again, with Donald Trump adopting it as one of the pillars of his campaign and his presidency, and it is being weaponized by the right against the "woke" left.

The PC myth has a life cycle that starts with *grievance creation*, moves on to *fabrication,* and ends in *diversion*. First, it feeds an imaginary injustice, a siege mentality, fostering intolerance. Once this fear of a purge of an old order sets in, once it is mainstreamed, it creates a regressive backlash. The backlash then subsumes genuine problems, such as unequal rights for women or ethnic minorities, diverting attention to the phantom "legitimate concerns" of those who have been convinced that there is an assault on their values, culture, livelihoods, and even lives. When that view takes hold, it is sustained by an industry and a political establishment that thrive off feeding false narratives about the goals of political correctness and fabricating stories to fit that narrative.

Grievance Creation:
How the Political Correctness Myth Was Born

The origin of the term political correctness is benign. In the US Supreme Court in the late eighteenth century, it implied a social convention of language, of elite propriety in expression both for accuracy and good manners. When deciding on whether an individual can sue a state, the chief justice stated that the language protocol of plaintiff versus "The United States," instead of the "People of the United States," was not politically correct. The sovereignty and authority of the nation lies in the people and is derived from their collective authority. What started essentially as legal protocol became a cudgel with which to beat back basic advances toward constitutional equality.

The term lay dormant, evolving yet relatively uncontested until the post–civil rights era in the United States. Up to that point, in the heady flux of the 1960s, it was deployed by the right and the left, both using it to describe what each considered to be the "correct" political position, which made it a fluid term open to interpretation. Anti–Vietnam War riots, for example, were to the Republicans politically incorrect. On the left, supporting and upholding civil rights legislation was the politically correct position to hold. There was no ownership of the term by any political party, or ideology. It was even tossed around lightly in jest, oftentimes by people poking fun at their own earnestness. A feminist might shave her legs and then quip that the concession to a classic image of femininity was not politically correct. In that sense, politically correct is the progenitor of today's "woke." They are both terms that originally called for a raised awareness and ended up being used as mockery. As a criticism, it was the left who first used political correctness to chastise their own for being too dogmatic. It started as shorthand meaning to be disciplined and aware in one's politics, only to descend into a slur, an eye roll at being somehow holier-than-thou.

Early warping of the term can be traced to 1960s America during a time when rapid social change had its activist and ideological center around university campuses. A nascent movement of students and academics began to question the status quo. The profile of those who traditionally studied and taught at such elite institutions was beginning to change and become less white, middle class, straight, and male. As a result, campus politics became restive. Civil rights, the Vietnam War, and reproductive rights were all part of a hotbed of issues that exercised students in Berkeley on the west coast and at Cornell on the east. The American academic Nancy Baker Jones summarized that historical moment: "The appearance of a critical mass of people representing viewpoints that disagreed significantly with established views was, from the point of view of the right, a dangerous turn of events, representing an incursion of 'special interests' on a commonly accepted educational tradition of such long standing that it had come to be considered apolitical, neutral, and universal." Those special interests were accused of leveraging political correctness to get their way.

By the 1980s, the term was beginning to become perverted and take on the shape familiar today—a right-wing labeling of the left as totalitarian in its patrolling of language, thought, and, by extension, ideology.

Today, alongside "woke" as a derivative insult of PC sits "virtue signaling" (i.e., motivated by showing off one's correct politics) as a criticism. But I can tell you from personal experience that these words and phrases are also *dog whistles*. I didn't quite understand why I, as opposed to others of different backgrounds, was accused of these things. Relatively little of my writing is on race and identity, but it is assumed that I am a race grifter, someone who pretends to be discriminated against for money. The same is assumed of other writers and journalists of color whenever they make the most rudimentary of noises about inequality. The point of these accusations is to portray people of color as essentially immoral and talentless, so they must advance their careers and cases by claiming victimhood.

Victim claiming

Merely saying the left is bossy and controlling isn't enough to convert people to the anti-PC cause. The right needed victims. More specifically, it needed to take victimhood away from those legitimately suffering. From African Americans demanding affirmative action to redress the structural imbalances of slavery, from women who demanded freedom from sexual harassment and workplace discrimination, from ethnic minorities who demanded freedom from racial slurs. There is a line that runs through conservative resistance to change, and it is the appropriation of victimhood from the weak by the powerful. Unable to come up with any reasons for that victimhood that are related to identity—being white, male, heterosexual, or part of a majority ethnic group doesn't throw up much opportunity for identity-based outrage—anti-PC critics chose a different route. Men, white people, and straight people were being victimized because those with less power than them had been *over*-empowered, creating a new system of oppression. All the toxic myths that underpin our age of discontent start out with this premise. It's all *gone too far*. Feminists, anti-racists, honest appraisers of history, all drunk with power, purging the old order. #MeToo had gone too far before its main villains had even stepped in court. Like the old adage about how quickly a lie travels halfway across the world, with myths, the powerful are already weeping before their victims have got their boots on.

In 1992, Robert Weissberg, a political scientist at the University of Illinois, wrote that conservatives were "the queers" of the '90s, living in fear of being outed for their political views, which had become so stigmatized that being a conservative was seen as no different from being a serial killer.

The victim claiming by PC critics asserts that the backlash is a natural one, that the polity simply doesn't like being nannied, doesn't like being told how to speak and what to say. But like all myths, its seeds are sown and tended by those who have an interest in maintaining things as they are. The negative branding of political correctness was a win for those forces, the culmination of a coordinated, well-funded campaign waged by the right since the 1970s. It began with the academy.

Follow the money

A cluster of conservative interests identified colleges and liberal academic institutions as the hub of civil rights activism, an anti-establishment cultural engine room. To neutralize the power of this new emerging revolutionary force, wealthy conservatives seeded several new think tanks and institutes. The latter were essentially civilian versions of military academies set up to incubate and train ground troops in a war against liberalism and then launch them into the nation's media, academia, and publishing world. These donors then purchased their way into the academy itself by funding graduate fellowships and scholarships and setting up positions for teaching staff. Political correctness became one of the main themes that these new recruits hammered, driving at the point that this new orthodoxy was stifling free thought and intellectual inquiry. PC critics established what is now a familiar conservative technique, one you will recognize from the anti-lockdown protests that took place as COVID-19 was tearing through the United States in 2020. They cited "our unique American freedoms."

Powerful institutions that dominate the conservative landscape to this day had their origins in this 1970s countermovement. It was never just about esoteric academic principles. It was a panic, a pre-emptive strike. The fear was that if liberal and left-wing politics grew unchecked, it might result in the dismantling of the capitalist free-doms that American corporations and the business elite enjoyed. The mandating of unionization was a particular concern. The Heritage Foundation, one of the most influential conservative public policy bodies in the United States, was founded in 1973 by two conservative activists and the president of the Coors Brewing Company, the grand-son of its founder, Adolph Coors. Joseph Coors Sr. presided over the company when it was the target of a nationwide boycott prompted by the company's unrestrained hiring and employment practices that included forced lie detector tests with questions intended to deter-mine whether any of them might be "troublemakers."

The circle of interests that established the foundation was con-cerned with maintaining a right-wing ideological political climate, and by extension the protection of commercial profit. They coalesced around the Powell Memorandum, a confidential memo written only for the eyes of the US Chamber of Commerce. Entitled "Attack on the American Free Enterprise System," the memorandum laid out an anti-Communist and anti–New Deal plan for business to claw back ground that was being lost to consumer-empowering efforts such as Ralph Nader's investigation into the automotive industry, one that revealed Detroit's manufacturing practices to be unsafe. The author of the report, Lewis F. Powell Jr., was a Supreme Court justice who, until his appointment to the court, was a director on the Phillip Morris board. Such was his ardor for American free enter-prise that he tried to argue, with little success, that tobacco companies' denials that their products caused cancer should not be dismissed as this was an infringement of their First Amendment rights. The foundation's stated mission is to "formulate and promote conservative public policies based on the principles of free enterprise, limited government, individual freedom, traditional American values, and a strong national defense."

The Cato Institute, one of the most influential free market–promoting think tanks—and one that objects to being classed as "conservative"—was also founded in the 1970s, and has invested heavily in releasing papers, studies, and peer-reviewed academic journals. This institute manages its media profile extremely carefully, positioning itself as a neutral player in the *marketplace of ideas*. Institutes like these play such a large role in American politics that they eventually become indistinguishable from lobbies or political parties. It is a phenomenon unique to the United States. A combination of a large war chest of corporate funds and a blurring of the lines between the academic and the ideological has turned intellectual life into a battleground disguised as good faith discourse.

The "libertarian" Cato Institute is effectively a conservative lobby group that pushes research papers and books into the hands of national editors and places guests onto the panels of national media. Its funding comes from the Koch brothers—billionaires and majority owners of Koch Industries, the second-largest privately held company in the United States. The network of conservative promotion lobbies and organizations they have created is so well funded and sophisticated that it serves almost as a shadow Republican Party. Over the past decades, the Koch brothers have, via their funds, campaigned effectively against expanding the government's role in healthcare and against climate change.

According to a 2010 *New Yorker* profile, the Kochs were "long-time libertarians who believe in drastically lower personal and corporate taxes, minimal social services for the needy, and much less oversight of industry—especially environmental regulation." The brothers funded so many campaigns against Obama administration policies that their ideological network came to be known as the "Kochtopus." Right-wing think tanks and lobbyists are slick organizations. There is no shouting, there are no undignified displays of anger in televised debates or at meetings, and there is no spectacle. The purpose is not to disrupt but to disseminate. Their premises are usually bland and faceless, with elaborate logos and generic names. The job titles of those they employ are both pompous and neutral, the kind of titles that children would come up with in a game of office make-believe. Take one of the Cato Institute's symposia on the subject of political correctness, held in November 2017. The institute put together a policy forum entitled "Marxist Origins of Hate-Speech Legislation and Political Correctness." Speakers included Christina Hoff Sommers, Resident Scholar at the American Enterprise Institute; Flemming Rose, Senior Fellow at the Cato Institute; and a moderator, Marian L. Tupy, Senior Policy Analyst at the Center for Global Liberty and Prosperity, also at the Cato Institute. All of these individuals were affiliated with a policy-promoting organization, but their elaborate titles made the event seem like a detached academic exercise and, more crucially, perfectly legitimate.

The Heritage Foundation is particularly obsessed with political correctness and has been since its inception. In 1991, the foundation published a report entitled "Political Correctness and the Suicide of the Intellect," which criticizes affirmative action because "two wrongs don't make a right." "We mustn't let things get by that we know are wrong," it concludes. "We must start to raise a little hell." Searching the foundation's site for articles containing the phrase "political correctness" throws up 13,839 results since the dawn of the web in the early 1990s. That's an average of 461 posts a year, or 1.3 a day. The foundation is churning out anti-PC propaganda on a daily basis.

Other organizations practically sponsored public "intellectuals" into being. Dinesh D'Souza, one of the most successful far-right conservative commentators in the US, was positively incubated by them. He started his career as editor of the *Dartmouth Review* in the early 1980s. At the time, the paper harassed an African American faculty member and published a criticism of affirmative action that was so racist in tone that it pierced the niche bubble of academic discourse to capture nationwide attention. The *Review* was receiving thousands of dollars from the rightist John M. Olin Foundation, which also sponsored D'Souza during a stint at the American Enterprise Institute, the end result of which was a book about illiberalism.

Funding grievance is a costly business. The successful smearing of PC was the culmination of an intellectual arms race that needed serious capital backing, capital that could afford to be nonprofit. Books, pamphlets, and strategically placed stories in the media pumped the idea of political correctness as a scourge into the public consciousness. MIT professor Ruth Perry, who was a student and activist in the 1960s and 1970s, told me that the majority of these stories were simply "a pack of lies." But these lies were disseminated by a machine that had considerable funding and therefore, profound reach.

By the early 1990s, the die was cast. Anti-PC academics, writers, talking heads, analysts, and researchers had spent three decades creating the PC panic myth. Their body of work frames much of the way we talk about politics today. Contemporary political discourse is rooted in a false dichotomy between freedom and control, one carefully constructed by anti-PC laborers and their funders. They were so successful that the final output wasn't just the discrediting of a raft of measures and language modulation. The PC campaign went beyond a fight against affirmative action or allowing transgender students to use the facilities of their choosing. Being anti-PC became tied up in notions of strength, robustness, masculinity, disdain for authority, in the belief that the American citizen is an individual sovereign who is the final arbiter of moral and legal judgments, regardless of the impact that has on their fellows. To trash political correctness effectively, you have to tear up the social contract. This is why America is the only country in the world where, during the early stages of its COVID-19 lockdown, Michigan protestors demanded isolation measures end so that they could get their hair cut. If it means others, or even they, catch COVID-19 and die . . . well, that's freedom. Anything else is political correctness. What started out as high respect and protocol with which to address the body of people that constitutes the United States of America in a way that was "politically correct" ended up as a way to demean it.

The point of tracing this history is to demonstrate that political correctness as a concept was exaggerated, then maligned, then used to poison political discourse and tip popular opinion in a conservative direction. It was not a process that happened spontaneously or as a result of any popular, cultural pushback. In 1995, academic John K. Wilson was on to the confected nature of the assault. "The attacks on political correctness did not arise from grassroots movements of noble individuals resisting leftist totalitarians," he wrote. "Instead they were carefully developed over many years by well-funded conservative groups."

Bearing fruit

The juggernaut of anti-PC campaigning deliberately overestimates the reach and influence of political correctness. Exaggeration is always the way with myth creation. The instant a demand for equality threatens to become mainstream, it is immediately abhorred as too much, an overreach. As far back as 1992, Ruth Perry wrote that "no sooner was it invoked as a genuine standard for sociopolitical practice—so that we might live as if the revolution has already happened—than it was mocked as purist, ideologically rigid and authoritarian."

Perry, who presciently wrote about how political correctness was being weaponized in the early 1990s, recalls when she first noticed that such a machine existed, when the effort began to bear fruit. "It was in the early eighties," she said, still clearly indignant at the underhand methods that were used almost forty years ago. "The right started to wage a culture war where they funded a lot of people to develop ideas. When TV or radio hosts discussed a topic such as feminism, for example, they would ask a normal academic type and a funded guest, who was only there to promote policy in line with their funders." She told me stories of campaigns on campus to discredit her and her female colleagues, libelous articles in the press, and intimidation tactics. Strange things began to happen. A right-wing newspaper appeared on campus overnight. When Perry started lecturing, someone who was not a student began to appear at her classes and take notes. Instrumental to this campaign was funding. By its very nature, the political left was not aligned with the interests of large corporations and multibillionaires. The fightback was left to academics, students, and activists who had not a fraction of the funding, nor therefore the reach, of the anti-PC right. They didn't stand a chance. Inevitably, the money and concerted campaign waged through the 1970s and 1980s, one which was met with little resistance of equal penetration from the left into the opinion-forming media, had successfully turned political correctness, on invented grounds, into an effective weapon that was being deployed by the White House itself.

By 1991, the right wing in the United States had elevated the concern of political correctness as a crisis of orthodoxy in thought to the presidency. In a commencement speech at the University of Michigan, then president George H. W. Bush declared: "The notion of political correctness has ignited controversy across the land. And although the movement arises from the laudable desire to sweep away the debris of racism and sexism and hatred, it replaces old prejudice with new ones."

These "new" prejudices, those that flip the hierarchy in favor of women, people of color, and those who are "other" in general, are in fact old, and not prejudices at all. They are merely an attempt to forge a new social order, one which cannot coexist with the old and its inbuilt inequalities. One of the difficulties of addressing concerns about political correctness is that the term's definition has been hijacked by those who now use it to mean anything they want, as long as it denotes something negative. Pejoratively, it is used by those who have a vested interest in maintaining a system that needs reform, who refuse to acknowledge that the system does not serve everyone equally. According to journalist Amanda Taub, writing for the *Vox* news website in 2015: "Political correctness . . . is a catch-all term we apply to people who ask for more sensitivity to a particular cause than we're willing to give—a way to dismiss issues as frivolous in order to justify ignoring them."

The moment these requests for sensitivity are made, they are, according to the establishment, an outrageous demand. Whether it was the civil rights movement in the 1960s or the theoretical right of a single trans student to use the female facilities in a school, the most tentative of steps toward redressing imbalance are always seen as going over the top. The primary motivator of myths is this fear of the pendulum swinging too far the other way, toward a matriarchy that persecutes men, toward a tyranny of people of color over white people, toward gay over straight, immigrant over native. Dominant groups have only maintained their power via oppression, so they cannot countenance a world where more rights for others means simply more equality, and not just a new system of oppression.

George H. W. Bush's "new" prejudices are, to their critics, always shifting and expanding. They have come to encompass everything from demanding that people be polite in their speech and manner toward others, to accommodating the sensitivities and needs of those for whom mainstream society had not been designed to cater. The myth—that there is such a thing as "going too far"—has displayed remarkable plasticity, morphing from an esoteric guide to manners, to an accusation of dishonesty and even conspiracy. Its danger is in not only creating resistance to change, but in fortifying the status quo against change. Under Donald Trump, the myth mutated once more. Political correctness became anything that conformed to convention, no matter how anodyne and sensible that convention is. Defying something as political correctness became nothing more than a childish, and dangerous, urge simply not to conform. It became the rationale behind not wearing a mask in a pandemic, and behind mocking those who do.

Political correctness as dog whistle

The role of political correctness as oppressor of thought and behavior was a pillar of Donald Trump's 2016 US election campaign. His elevation as some sort of truth teller, the embodiment of free speech—we will come to that in the next chapter—breaking free from the shackles of mind control, is a master class in how myths are leveraged in order to maintain power structures or, in some cases, reinstate them.

Research published in May 2017 by the *Journal of Social and Political Psychology* found a strong correlation between the belief that there were new restrictive standards on language and support for Trump. In a poll of his supporters, this belief, rather than ideology as such, was a more reliable predictor of support for the president.

"At a general level," the report observes, "evidence suggests that Trump's grandiose rhetorical style was one of the reasons he won the Republican primary. Further and more specifically, polls from the election cycle suggested that people liked his provocative language and that feeling voiceless better predicted Trump support than multiple other variables, some of which include age, race, and attitudes toward Muslims, illegal immigrants, and Hispanics." The research further showed the extent of the problem by coming to an interesting conclusion, one that absolved Trump voters of any sinister motivations for disliking political correctness. What they displayed was apparently just a natural reaction to the "norms of restrictive communication." This is the deeply buried seed of grievance creation, the idea that managing speech or behavior, something humans do organically all the time in order for society to function, is somehow unnatural when it comes to PC. The question that needs to be asked is why did Trump voters feel like those norms were so oppressive to them? Who decided that those norms were "restrictive"? And if indeed these norms are oppressive, what is it that lies beneath, and which we must allow to be expressed if we are to prevent this reportedly inevitable backlash?

What lies beneath was hinted at by Donald Trump on the campaign trail when he defended his history of verbally abusing women. "I think the big problem this country has is being politically correct," Trump said, to audience applause. "I've been challenged by so many people, I don't frankly have time for total political correctness. And to be honest with you, this country doesn't have time either."

Trump was right. The country didn't have "time" for political correctness. The impatience and frustration in not having time is a reaction to the demands made on people to be decent, to respect their fellow citizens, to put in the effort and the *time* to learn how to treat others with dignity. It is a rejection of that expectation. A stamping of the foot. Others should remain othered. They should remain in their place and not presume that they have the right to change how Americans talk, think, or behave. There is an implicit anger of insult in not having time for political correctness, perhaps even of humiliation. Those who reject political correctness with such vehemence are reasserting their status in a country where their status has been a given for far too long. Political correctness to the

PC rebels is a threat, a window into the future where their failures and inadequacies will no longer be neutralized by their privileges. And so, the rebels dismiss and smear those who demand that they give up their unearned equity.

"Having elevated the powers of PC to mythic status," wrote academic Moira Weigel, "the draft-dodging billionaire, son of a slumlord, taunted the parents of a fallen soldier and claimed that his cruelty and malice was, in fact, courage." Courage for speaking truths when no one else dared to.

There is a history of maligning those campaigning for political equality as elitist, out of touch, effete snobs who were getting in the way of serious governance. Such a strategy played (and still plays) very well with the voting public.

In his 1966 campaign for governor of California, Ronald Reagan attacked Berkeley protestors, claiming that "a small minority of beatniks, radicals, and filthy speech advocates have brought such shame to a great university." A year later, Nixon attacked university activism as "elitist" and "morally relativist." The year after, presidential nominee George Wallace said on the campaign trail that he was speaking on behalf of the "workin' folk fed up with bureaucrats in Washington, pointy-headed intellectuals, swaydo [sic] intellectual morons tellin' 'em how to live their lives." These addresses were the progenitors of today's sneers about "safe spaces," "trigger warnings," and "microaggressions." All three were saying what Trump said in 2016: they had no time for political correctness, and neither did the country—they just did not have a name for it yet.

The agitation against some amorphous, elitist enemy imposing their ways on "workin' folk" waxes and wanes according to what sort of consensus conservative forces need to create. When first Gulf War–era president George H. W. Bush invoked PC, it was not a coincidence that the last time there was a need to mention "new prejudices" that were not aligned with the needs of the government of the day, was during the Vietnam War. The undesirable political correctness of the early 1990s was one that would not accept the old way of doing things, where patrician white men with a penchant for foreign wars could count on the jingoism of American exceptionalism to cheer them on. A lack of uniformity breeds dissent, and so it is logical that diversity of thought becomes a threat. To bash academics, experts, politicians, bureaucrats, and members of the left-wing media as elitist, bleeding heart, out of touch, these are all sublimated ways of saying political correctness as a whole is the enemy, that it is the cautious calculation of the mind attempting to take over the authentic feeling of the heart. Once this feeling is settled, it's only a matter of time before it turns into full-blown paranoia.

By 2016, the myth of political correctness had so taken hold that the grievance boil it had been nourishing for years finally burst. In 2017 and 2018, US attorney general Jeff Sessions made two speeches in which he said that colleges were creating a generation of "sanctimonious, sensitive, supercilious snowflakes" and that campuses were an "echo chamber of political correctness and homogenous thought, a shelter for fragile egos." During one of those speeches, the crowd began to chant "lock her up" in reference to Hillary Clinton—presumably to demonstrate that there were no "snowflakes" among them.

Fabrication—The Virus Is a Hoax

When political correctness is associated with weakness and submission, its critics harness the power of fear—fear that liberals want to control the populace. And when the charge of political correctness has been used for decades as a way to dismiss ideas or people, eventually it will be used to manipulate ideas and people.

Such manipulation can be a matter of life and death. The initial impulse of the US presidential administration when the coronavirus pandemic hit was to minimize and evade. The right-wing media and intellectual infrastructure helped in this cause. The same machine that whips up outrage over imagined threats from a transgender student just existing in a school can easily mobilize to discredit threats that are real.

Trump, having had success with his PC labels during his first election campaign, delayed a serious response to the pandemic, then undermined that response by deciding that any measures to halt the spread of the virus and save lives were "politically correct." From the beginning he dismissed COVID-19 as a Chinese problem, one which wouldn't affect Americans. To suggest otherwise was being politically correct. Then he sneered at mask wearing and social distancing. Both were politically correct and thus not required. Finally, in withdrawing support from the World Health Organization, Trump decided that the WHO had "put political correctness above life-saving measures."

The fabrication network kicked into gear. Jiore Craig, who studies the spread of disinformation online, told the *Cut* that after a period of confusion among right and alt-right outlets and pundits, partisans gratefully adopted this anti-PC line of assault.

"They've landed on attacking the left about 'PC culture'—arguing that the left is more worried about the racist phrasing Trump uses for the virus than about the virus itself. That's an example of something they've unified on since last week, because they know this playbook; they know how to attack the left on PC culture; they can run with that."

The signal from the top was picked up by a portion of the population that had grown up on a diet of political correctness–bashing by what appeared to be respectable authoritative figures. They followed Trump's and the media's cue. Another group of players—from a law firm staffed by former Trump White House officials, Tea Party protest organizers, and a loose affiliation of conservative influencers called Save Our Country—then took the PC messaging and ran with it, folding it into larger narratives about government overreach. The result was a string of protests in which Americans put themselves in harm's way, ignored social distancing, refused to wear masks, and demanded that the country reopen. Cell phone data from these anti-lockdown protests shows that demonstrators, some of whom attended events connected with COVID-19 cases, traveled hundreds of miles, crossed into different states, and raised the risk of spreading the virus to areas that had few infections. According to a report entitled "Black Lives Matter, Social Distancing and COVID-19" by the National Bureau of Economic Research, Black Lives Matter protests that happened later in 2020, in contrast, did not lead to a spike in infections. Officials in the city of Minneapolis told the *Washington Post*: "The low infection rates reflect that the protests were outside, that most people wore masks and that people spent most of their time in motion, circulating through the crowd."

The anti-lockdown protests were a prototype of the astroturfing by the anti-PC industry. Rather than being spontaneous grass roots objections, these demonstrations were provoked by coordinated political messaging, and then their practicalities were organized by behind-the-scenes figures. The victimhood-stealing tactic was clear here too. An economic adviser for the White House compared the protestors to Rosa Parks. Trump said that it was a strong statement, but "I understand where he's coming from." Some of these latter-day Rosa Parks activists held up Nazi slogans.

The Tool—Diversion and Frequency Scrambling

The most effective myths tend to come with a clever technical tool that not only denies reality but prevents a discussion about reality. In the case of political correctness, it is *frequency scrambling*, a technique which uses the concept of political correctness for diversion, to distort the conversation and move it away from what it is people are fundamentally objecting to.

This form of diversion is a favorite among Islamophobes, so easy is it to hide prejudice against Muslims behind rising fears of Islamic terrorism. A case in point is that of Park51, or as it came to be known in public discussion, the "Ground Zero mosque." The first media mention for the center, which included a memorial to 9/11 victims, appeared in the *New York Times* in 2009. Moderate media attention to what was essentially a community center intensified after conservative figures Pamela Geller and Robert Spencer, founders of "Stop Islamization of America," launched a campaign opposing the construction, giving it the "Ground Zero mosque" name. The plans for the project had gone through the regular channels and in 2010 were unanimously approved by the Lower Manhattan Development Board.

It wasn't long before political correctness came into it. President Obama's refusal to condemn the project was seen by some as an endorsement, a position that inevitably revealed his Islamist sympathies. Others presented it as a capitulation to pressure. Republican US representative Peter King said in a statement that "while the Muslim community has the right to build the mosque they are abusing that right by needlessly offending so many people who have suffered so much." They should have been pushed by Barack Obama to move on, he continued. "The right and moral thing for President Obama to have done was to urge Muslim leaders to respect the families of those who died and move their mosque away from Ground Zero. Unfortunately, the president caved into political correctness."

Political correctness isn't just a way of behaving. It's a pressure, something someone "caves in to," a minefield that one navigates, afraid of a wrong move. Leveraging convenient sympathy and concern for the well-being of 9/11 victims' families, the Park51 critics shifted the conversation from whether a group should have the right to build a community center—everyone agreed they did indeed have the right—to a straw man in which it was suggested that Muslims intended to build a shrine to 9/11 terrorists on Ground Zero and Barack Obama was too cowed by the PC police to stop them.

Another high-profile figure who had shown slim regard for the 9/11 victims (and boasted that one of his buildings was now the tallest in downtown Manhattan after the Twin Towers were leveled) also suddenly felt a surge of sympathy. Once it appeared that a Muslim communal space would be built near Ground Zero, Donald Trump wrote, "The Ground Zero Mosque should not go up where planned. It is wrong. My offer still stands to buy the property. Good deal for everyone."

These debates also claim that there is disproportionate attention paid to minority demands at the expense of the white working class. But just like the fake pearl clutch of the Ground Zero mosque, the concern for white working classes by PC critics seems only to arise when it can be used as a cudgel. This is frequency scrambling. The technique diverts us from a genuine grievance by raising a false one. So much time is then spent on rebutting the false grievance—Obama's silence was not an endorsement; the mosque is no shrine to terrorists; it's not even a mosque—that no time at all is then spent on the original complaint, which is that every American enjoys the right to build and worship as they please.

The time that I have spent writing these words is, ironically, a triumph of frequency scrambling, in that this chapter is dedicated to rebutting false allegations of political correctness, but the myth is so deeply ingrained that first it must be dispelled before the facts can be argued.

Every time an issue is presented as one of PC, the air is sucked out of it and it cannot catch fire. If minorities demand some form of affirmative action, we end up discussing the non-minorities who might be victimized as a result, as opposed to the reasons affirmative action is needed in the first place. If women demand a new way of speaking to and about them in the workplace, we end up discussing the men who will be bewildered and prone to victimization, rather than why women have made the demand in the first place. Diversion is a tool that depends on couching demands in terms of their impact on others, rather than their inherent merit. It is a technique that stresses excess—PC is unnatural and is asking for too much, just like feminism—and purloins victimhood from its rightful owners.

This is necessary to provide cover for the next component of the myth.

Political correctness as sanction

The myth of a political correctness crisis serves many purposes. It dampens efforts for change by repackaging these efforts as assaults. It gives people license to disrespect rational guidance and behave selfishly in social crises such as pandemics. But its most valuable purpose is its moral shield, a get-out-of-jail card for those who hold intolerant views but who do not wish to be held accountable for those views, or even to feel bad about them.

This is why "you can't say anything anymore" is such a frequently deployed defense by those who make prejudiced statements. Their argument is not that their opinions are bigoted, it's that they have been wrongly stigmatized.

In 2017, while reporting on Trump's supporters' unconditional loyalty, the *Atlantic*'s Adam Serwer came across a frequent excuse for Trump's racism. "I believe that everybody has a right to be in the United States no matter what your color, no matter what your race, your religion, what sex you prefer to be with, so I'm not against that at all, but I think that some of us just say racial statements without even thinking about it," a Pennsylvania woman told him. But when pressed on Trump's comments on race and Islam she said: "I think the other party likes to blow it out of proportion and kind of twist his words, but what he says is what he means, and it's what a lot of us are thinking."

This is the most common response to any queries about Trump's sexism, racism, or Islamophobia. In 2018, I interviewed members of a large, second-generation Irish American family of Trump supporters from New Jersey who rattled off variations on the same theme—it was how Trump's comments and behavior were received that was the problem.

Trump's sexist comments were "locker room talk"; his racist comments were not racist at all, he was just stating "what we all were thinking"; his abuse of, and aggression toward, the media and political opponents was "straight talk." Hillary Clinton came up often as the sinister, politically correct analog to Trump. "You don't know what she's thinking," the matriarch of the family said. "You can't trust her, because she's trying to be politically correct all the time." When it came to Islam, they were taking no prisoners. When I put it to them that I, as a Sudanese citizen, would be banned from visiting the US under Trump's Muslim ban, they did not even try to pretend that it wasn't a Muslim ban—a common fig leaf is that if it were a Muslim ban if would cover all Muslim countries, not just the few that it does. "If you want to keep the bad ones out, you've got to keep the good ones out as well," came the answer. They felt it was, indeed, brave of Trump to go against what they perceived to be the pressure of political correctness.

This is the final stage of PC as sanction, to make those who are anti-PC feel not only that they have been victimized, but that they are, in fact, brave to go against this imaginary tide. It's an impressive mental contortion that is only possible because there is so much invested in it—the preservation of status, the need for impunity, the projection of collective grievance onto a single convenient source, the flattering of the self.

A model of this thought pattern, one which ends inevitably in the normalization of extremely problematic views, is author Sam Harris's 2017 reanimation of the IQ race wars that began with the publication of *The Bell Curve* in 1994. That book's authors, psychologist Richard J. Herrnstein and political scientist Charles Murray, argue that intelligence is a mixture of social and genetic factors, making assertions about racial differences in IQ that critics say irresponsibly discount environmental factors.

Harris came to an epiphany. He realized his earlier dismissal of Charles Murray's views that certain races have naturally higher or lower IQs was a product of groupthink and he decided to rectify his error by hosting Murray on his podcast. "Unfortunately," Harris concluded, "the controversy over *The Bell Curve* did not result from legitimate, good-faith criticisms of its major claims. Rather, it was the product of a politically correct moral panic that totally engulfed Murray's career and has yet to release him."

Once Harris summoned political correctness, he immediately cast himself as a lone crusader pursuing a pioneering and taboo subject, "forbidden knowledge," he calls it. But in fact, as Ezra Klein observed in *Vox*: "This isn't 'forbidden knowledge.' It's ancient prejudice. . . . For two white men to spend a few hours discussing why black Americans are, as a group, less intelligent than whites isn't a courageous stand in the context of American history; it's a common one."

The timing is important to note. A work that for decades had been consigned to the fringes of respectable debate just happens to be enjoying a renaissance at a time where false equivalence and the notion of PC as cover for regressive views is in the ascendance. This is no coincidence. Harris does not just happen to be fitting in with the zeitgeist, one where if a thing has not been entertained—racial differences, biological differences between men and women—then it must be entertained, regardless of why it was dismissed or marginalized in the first place. Anything else, to borrow Harris's words, is "moral cowardice."

Harris often refers to "bad faith" when discussing his critics. He claims that they approach his positions with prior assumptions about his intentions and therefore will not engage in honest discussions about what he is arguing. So in good faith, I would suggest that Harris is not in fact a racist who would like to establish that there are genetic differences between races that cannot be accounted for by anything other than genetics. I would suggest that he is a narcissist: he is in love with his vision of himself as a PC warrior. The allure of the PC warrior is sometimes too strong to resist for those who view themselves as brave arbiters of truth. PC knights are having a moment in popular discourse. They make up an entire cohort, feted in the *New York Times* as members of an "intellectual dark web" that is making "an end run around the mainstream conversation." They are also joined by liberals who have succumbed to the grandiosity of defending liberal values. *New York* magazine's Jonathan Chait obsesses about American free-speech campus controversies, even when he reluctantly admits campus scuffles might be small fry in the grand scheme of things and have been occurring for some time now without bringing about fascism. But this will not stop him from presenting them as part of a great threat to liberalism.

There is something unavoidably macho about the language around political correctness, which is often expressed in terms of strength and weakness. Those who care about abusive language, racial and sexist slurs, and so on, are weak, thin-skinned, demanding that we go against nature by overregulating and policing innocent and inevitable human behavior. The implication is that to indulge political correctness is to create a sort of artificial state of oppression, where humans cannot exercise discretion or shrug things off. At the heart of this is the kind of biological determinism that assumes that just because some things occur in nature, e.g. suspicion of other races due to group-preservation instincts, that means that they should be accepted. This biological argument, strangely, is rarely made about violent crime or child abuse, both things that have occurred in nature since record keeping began.

Branding PC as oversensitive, elitist, inauthentic, and oppressive has been so successful that defending it has become toxic for the left. Right-wing populists have painted the left as out of touch; it cannot afford to play into the stereotype. This is why, when Hillary Clinton was interviewed by the *Guardian* newspaper in November 2018 on the topic of how to combat populism, her first suggestion was to curb immigration, because that is what "lit the flame." Her view was not that immigration was bad, rather that it was helping the right and must be jettisoned if the left is to be seen as on the side of the man on the street. Clinton's frequency was well and truly scrambled if her solution to populism is playing into the hands of the right by advocating its policies and mirroring its tactics. Frequency scrambling makes values negotiable.

The journalist Arwa Mahdawi calls this "populist correctness," which she describes as "the smearing and silencing of points of view by labeling them 'elitist'—and therefore at odds with the will of the people and the good of the country." In the United States, populist correctness has ironically enforced its own sort of orthodoxy on the right. In 2018, Georgia Republican gubernatorial candidate Brian Kemp's campaign ad was simply entitled "Offends." In it, he issues a series of dog whistles while wrapped in the cloak of plain talking.

"I'm Brian Kemp," he says, "and I believe in God, family and country—in that order. I say, 'Merry Christmas' and 'God bless you.' I strongly support President Trump, our troops, and ironclad borders. I stand for our national anthem. If any of this offends you, then I'm not your guy. If you're ready for a politically incorrect conservative who will end corrupt pay-to-play politics, I'm Brian Kemp, and I'm asking for your vote."

The man he was running against, a hard-core conservative by any standard, was caught on tape complaining that the gubernatorial nomination process had turned into a competition to show "who had the biggest gun, who had the biggest truck, and who could be the craziest." Two days after the "Offends" ad ran, Trump endorsed Brian Kemp. A few days later, Kemp won the GOP nomination for Georgia governor.

A week before, Ed Kilgore observed on the *Intelligencer* blog that "if Kemp wins his runoff on July 24 with this strategy, it is going to reinforce the already powerful Trumpian impulse to treat conservative 'base' voters as motivated above all by the desire to go back to the wonderful days when a white man could without repercussions tell a racist joke, 'tease' women about their physical appearance or sexual morals, and mock people who in some way (say, a disability) differ from one's own self." He wrote, "At some point we may all come to understand that it's not (except in some scattered college campuses) the politically correct who are imposing speech norms on the rest of us, but the politically incorrect who won't be happy until offending the less powerful is again recognized as among the principal Rights of Man." Or as the British writer Polly Toynbee put it, political correctness crisis mythology is used as "coded cover" for those who "still want to say Paki, spastic, or queer."

Growing pains

Edward Said described the origins of political correctness as not "a matter of replacing one set of authorities and dogmas with another, nor of substituting one center for another. It was always a matter of opening and participating in a central strand of intellectual and cultural effort and of showing what had always been, though indiscernibly, a part of it, like the work of women, or of blacks, and servants—but which had been either denied or derogated."

In this most basic form, as respect for others, as integrating the voices of the marginalized, political correctness has been hugely successful in regulating how we interact peacefully. From the 1980s onward, political correctness banished anti-Semitic and racial slurs from the public space and the mainstream media. It stigmatized homophobic language and went some distance in limiting language that demeaned or objectified women. The knock-on effect of this is an informing of behavior at best, and the creation of a safe and inclusive society for all. But this effort needed to be sustained by constant vigilance and structural reform, a sincere adoption of these norms into the political culture of a country. That follow-through did not happen, allowing an almost universal resignation to the fact that PC is a bad thing to go unchallenged. Nobody likes to be told what to think or how to behave, goes the argument, and look at the frustration that political correctness sowed? But this frustration isn't the failure of PC, it is a failure in arguing for the value of PC and enthusiastically promoting it with as much force as it was stigmatized with. Political correctness is not wrong, it is merely unfashionable. As the British broadcaster James O'Brien put it to those who resent having to suppress their offensive thoughts: "Where would you like your sewage? In the pipes underground or flowing in the streets?"

The reason political correctness met with resistance in 1960s America was that it pointed out that the existing state of affairs was artificially imposed via coercive political, racial, social, and economic forces rather than a natural flow that just found its level. In the 1990s, PC quickly became defined as an incursion by "special interests" because the establishment viewed itself as apolitical, neutral, and promoting universal values. The problem with dismissing political correctness—and here I'm using the term in its pre-1990s, non-pejorative form—is that doing so reinforces cultural entitlement. Only people who are not transgender, or do not care about a transgender person, can afford to dismiss Trump's military ban on transgender soldiers as a mere distraction. Only people who are not afraid that a person of color will be shot by the police on a whim can afford to dismiss Trump's racism as a "side issue." In a moral universe, political correctness would not be necessary at all. Until we achieve that moral universe, political correctness is a must. Likewise, in a homogenous universe, political correctness would not exist. In a diverse world, political correctness is the stretching, the expansion, and often the growing pains of a society enlarging to accommodate all its members.

The threat to social cohesion is not that there is too much political correctness, it is that there is not enough.

3

The Myth of the Free Speech Crisis

> Many Americans have a child-like understanding of freedom . . . as the absence of government.
>
> —*Anand Giridharadas*

I began writing in an online age. My first column was published in 2008 and I remember well how unprepared I was for the comments that began appearing underneath. From the beginning, there was no space between me and the reader, no intermediary, just an online "moderator" whose job it was to delete comments that violated the newspaper's terms of service. I remember walking away from the screen and taking a walk around the block to breathe through the nausea, then going back to read comments that sneered at my intelligence, honesty, and prose.

I got over it quickly. A few columns later, it seemed a futile exercise to worry about what an audience would think. Being from a generation that straddled the real and virtual worlds, I had an instinctive sense of which comments were valuable and which were not. The immediate feedback made the writing process twofold—action and reaction. I would engage with the commenters who made valid points and encourage those who I sensed had something interesting to say but who had become caught up in emotion to reread the piece and return. Sometimes I would react to those who were abusive in a calculatedly dismissive tone. It was like being a teacher in front of a difficult class, trying to encourage the good students while striking a balance with the disruptive ones, asserting authority but not dropping to their level.

In those days, comments on any given story were open for seventy-two hours. Coming to the close of a thread felt like mooring a ship after a few days on choppy waters, like an achievement, something that I and the readers had gone through together. We had discussed sensitive, complicated ideas about politics, race, gender, and sexuality and, at the end, via a rolling conversation, we had gotten somewhere.

In the decade since, the tenor of those comments became so personal and abusive that the ship was often scuttled before making it to shore—the moderators would simply shut the thread down. When it first started happening, I took it as a personal failure—perhaps I had not struck the right tone or had not sufficiently hedged all my points, provoking readers into thinking I was being dishonest or incendiary. After some time, it dawned on me that my writing was the same. It was the commenters who had changed. It was becoming harder to discuss almost anything without a virtual snarl in response. And it was becoming harder to be a part of those discussions and avoid the virtual snarl if one were not white or male.

As a result, the *Guardian* overhauled its policy and decided that it would not open comment threads on pieces that were certain to derail. Where some other columnists were relieved, to me it felt like giving up. I still feel a little stab of disappointment when I see that an article of mine is not open to comments. A couple of times, I even remonstrated with the moderators to change their minds, but they knew better than me. They had a duty of care to the writers, some of whom struggled with the abuse, and a duty of care to new writers who might succumb to a chilling effect if they knew that to embark on a journalism career nowadays involves suffering relentless online thuggery. Alongside these moral concerns there were also practical, commercial ones. There were simply not enough resources to manage all the open threads at the same time with the increased level of attention that was now required. These were all fair and sensible reasons. The ship was now not even setting sail. The commenters and I were stuck in port.

Over the past ten years, many platforms in the press and social media have had to grapple with the challenges of managing users with increasingly sharp and offensive tones while maintaining enough space for maximum expression, feedback, and interaction. Speech has never been more free, or less mediated. Anyone with internet access can create a profile and write, tweet, blog, or comment, with little vetting and no hurdle of technological skill. But the primary losers in this growth of expression, have been women, minorities, and LGBTQ+ people. A 2017 Pew survey revealed that a "wide cross section" of Americans experience online abuse, but that the majority of it was directed toward minorities, with a quarter of black Americans saying they have been attacked online due to race or ethnicity. Ten percent of Hispanics and 3 percent of whites reported the same. Abuse of women on Twitter was at the epicenter of this new storm of online violence. Hostility toward women online is so intense that it has amounted to a human rights crisis, according to Amnesty International. But the nature of the abuse women face online, particularly on Twitter, is qualitatively different from the abuse received by minorities, in that it comes with the tangible threat of violence and stalking by both familiar and anonymous users. The US organization National Network to End Domestic Violence found that "97 percent of domestic violence programs reported that abusers use technology to stalk, harass, and control victims." In the UK, Women's Aid reported that 85 percent of abuse victims said the abuse they received online from partners or former partners mirrored the abuse pattern offline. Half of the women polled said that online abuse came with explicit threats of violence.

Being black, Muslim, and a woman with a minor public profile online meant I had a front-row seat to the genesis and development of this epidemic of virtual harassment which often spilled out into real life.

The vast majority of this assault not only goes unpunished, it is positively encouraged by the very business models of the tech platforms that host abusive users. Still, it is somehow conventional wisdom that free speech is under assault in a new "cancel culture" that hunts people accused of not toeing politically correct orthodoxies, that college campuses have succumbed to an epidemic of *no-platforming*, that social media mobs are ready to raise their pitchforks at the most innocent slip of the tongue or joke, and that Enlightenment values that protected the right to free expression and individual liberty are under threat. The cause of this, it is claimed, is a liberal totalitarianism that is the result of intolerance and thin skin. This tyranny is allegedly fascist in its brutal inclinations to silence the individual while acting as a refuge for the weak, the easily wounded, and the coddled. Instead of reckoning with the rise in online abuse, hate speech, and hate crime against minorities and women, we spend much of our time panicking about a fictional cancel culture that in many cases is just "consequence culture."

This is the myth of the free speech crisis. It is an extension of the political correctness myth but is a recent mutation more specifically linked to efforts or impulses to normalize hate speech or shut down legitimate responses to it. The purpose of the myth is not to secure freedom of speech, that is, the right to express one's opinions without censorship, restraint, or legal penalty. The purpose is to secure the license to speak with impunity; not freedom of expression, but rather freedom from the consequences of that expression.

The myth has two components: the first is that all speech should be free; the second is that freedom of speech means freedom from objection. On the first, I'll cut to the chase. Not all speech should be free. It's hard to argue that. I always feel slightly sheepish or apologetic when I have to be blunt and just say there are, and should be, severe restrictions on speech. Instinctively it feels wrong to ask that we have less freedom of speech—to be unmoved when people with views you disagree with are silenced or banned smacks of illiberalism. And it's hard to argue for less freedom in the society in which I live, because is it not the logical conclusion that limiting rights of expression will catch up with me at some point? Will it not be me one day, on the wrong side of free speech?

A kernel of something makes all myths stick, something that speaks to a sense of justice and liberty, and to due process. It gives them an openness that appeals to the good and well-intentioned while making them vulnerable to cynical manipulation. But challenging the myth of a free speech crisis does not mean enabling the state to police and censor even further. Moreover, there is no need to challenge the crisis because no such crisis exists. The freedom of speech crisis myth's purpose is to guilt people into conceding their right of response to attack and to destigmatize racism and prejudice. It aims to blackmail good people into ceding space to bad ideas, even though they have a legitimate right to refuse. And it is a myth that demands, in turn, its own silencing and an undermining of individual freedom. To accept the freedom of speech crisis myth is to give up your own right to turn off the comments when they become toxic.

The myth and its promoters thrive on cognitive dissonances and good intentions, feeding them with *free speech absolutism*, invoking a nonexistent marketplace of ideas, fabrication of free speech scandals, and *slippery slope* fallacies.

Speech Is Free But Not Absolute

There are many things that people do and can say in public, with little fear of legal intervention from the state. But there are always limits and always should be. This applies to almost all human behavior in secular, democratic societies. The most straightforward example is how we dress. Broadly we can wear what we want, but most people will stay within the confines of social custom because otherwise a judgment may be made about their character or they may offend others. Men will generally wear a tie to a funeral; women will limit more revealing clothes to their social, rather than professional lives. Where social custom fails, the state intervenes. There are legal limits in even the most permissive societies on public nudity, while legislation against the wearing of the burqa and the niqab is gathering momentum in Europe. In France, both the burqa and revealing one's private parts are banned. And in countries where there are few explicit laws on dress, people still tend to fall back on customary behavior even when there is no legal threat of punishment. In Germany, nudity is legal, as is the burqa, but there is no preponderance of either.

Free speech, like public dress codes, is not an abstract notion, it has a purpose; it is a regulator of interaction, rather than an end in itself. It sets specific parameters.

In its most pure form freedom of speech serves two purposes: protection from state prosecution when challenging authority or orthodoxy; and the protection of fellow citizens from the damaging consequences of absolute—completely, legally unregulated—speech such as slander. According to Francis Canavan in *Freedom of Expression: Purpose as Limit*, his analysis of the most permissive free speech law, the First Amendment to the US Constitution, free speech must have a rational end, which is to facilitate communication between citizens. Where it does not serve that end, it is limited. Like all freedoms, it ends when it infringes upon the freedoms of others. The US Supreme Court itself "has never accepted an absolutist interpretation of freedom of speech. It has not protected, for example, libel, slander, perjury, false advertising, obscenity and profanity, solicitation of a crime, or 'fighting' words. The reason for their exclusion from First Amendment protection is that they have minimal or no values as ideas, communication of information, appeal to reason, step toward truth, etc.; in short, no value in regard to the ends of the Amendment."

Those who believe in the free speech crisis myth fail to make the distinction between "fighting" words and speech that facilitates communication, between free speech and absolute speech.

Using this litmus test, the first hint the free speech crisis is actually an absolute speech crisis arises from the issues it focuses on.

On college campuses, the "crisis" is overwhelmingly around race and gender. On social media, the free speech ax is wielded by trolls, Islamophobes, and misogynists, leading to an abuse epidemic that platforms have failed to curb. This free speech crisis movement has managed to stigmatize reasonable protest, which has existed for years without being branded "silencing" or being deemed an assault on free expression.

What is considered speech that is worthy of protection is broadly subjective and depends on the limits a society has agreed to draw. Western societies like to think of their version of freedom of speech as exceptionally pristine, but it is also tainted (or tempered, depending on where you're coming from) by convention. A good example of how there are, in fact, accepted curbs on freedom of speech, outside the limits of the law, and how they are in fact arbitrary, is the case of Milo Yiannopoulos.

Popularly known as Milo, a British university dropout and lapsed journalist, Yiannopoulos arrived in the public sphere in 2015 after joining Breitbart News and styling himself as a lightning rod for online campaigns against women and minorities. He believes that "feminism is a cancer" and that "rape culture is a myth." In 2016, he was permanently banned from Twitter for conducting a coordinated abuse campaign against US actor Leslie Jones. "With the cowardly suspension of my account," Milo stated, "Twitter has confirmed itself as a safe space for Muslim terrorists and Black Lives Matter extremists, but a no-go zone for conservatives."

In 2017, Simon & Schuster offered Milo a $250,000 advance for a book about his life. When faced with public outcry, the publisher defended its decision by releasing a statement in which it described Milo as simply someone with "controversial" opinions, who will take his place among their stable of other authors, many of whom are also "controversial," and who appeal to "many audiences of readers."

Calls for a boycott sent liberal free speech campaigners into an indignation of chivalry. Like the PC gone-too-far hysteria, concerns about a free speech crisis appeal to a certain type of classical liberal, one who is oblivious to how these moral panics are fabricated and manipulated by those with an agenda. This liberal is blinded by the eagerness to land generally on the right side of freedom and individual liberty. Led by the National Coalition Against Censorship, free speech advocates issued a statement in opposition to a nascent boycott of Milo Yiannopoulos's publisher, claiming that it will have "a chilling effect" on authors and publishers and will not prevent the spread of "noxious ideas." The statement, signed by, among others, Index on Censorship, the Authors' Guild, and the National Council of Teachers of English, said: "The suppression of noxious ideas does not defeat them; only vigorous disagreement can counter toxic speech effectively."

This chimed with Simon & Schuster's defense of the book deal. All ideas good or bad should be heard—that someone should buy them is, of course, the unspoken rule—Milo was just another flower in the flourishing garden of opinion. Who were Simon & Schuster to dictate what should be published and what should not? The company was just an intermediary between opinion maker and audience, that's all.

New information that came to light after this statement demonstrated that Simon & Schuster was a little more than a middleman. Most unfortunately for the publisher, later in the same year that Milo secured his book deal, footage emerged in which he endorsed pederasty. In a podcast called *The Drunken Peasants*, which aired in 2016,

Yiannopoulos commented: "We get hung up on this child abuse stuff." He said he believed the current legal age of consent was "probably about right" before saying that some teenagers are "capable" of consenting to sexual activity at a younger age.

It gets worse: "There are certainly people who are capable of giving consent at a younger age. I certainly consider myself to be one of them, people who were sexually active younger." This "particularly happens in the gay world," he added. Relationships between thirteen-year-olds and twenty-five- or twenty-eight-year-olds were fine, he specified. Consent was an "arbitrary and oppressive" idea, he said, "people are messy and complex, and in the homosexual world particularly, some of those relationships between younger boys and older men, the coming of age relationships" are places in which "those older men help those young boys to discover who they are and give them security and safety and provide them with love and a reliable rock when they can't speak to their parents."

This was too much even for one of the presenters of the podcast, who said in response: "This sounds like priest molestation to me." Milo replied: "And do you know what? I'm grateful to Father Michael, I wouldn't give nearly as good head if it wasn't for him."

Reader, the free speech winds turned. Milo was dropped by Simon & Schuster. The free speech campaigners fell silent. Condemnations and distancing and disavowals followed. He resigned from his position at Breitbart News.

Once Milo's book deal with the prestigious publishing house was rescinded, the writer Roxane Gay wrote:

When his comments about pedophilia/pederasty came to light,
Simon & Schuster realized it would cost them more money to

do business with Milo than he could earn for them. They did not finally "do the right thing" and now we know where their threshold, pun intended, lies. They were fine with his racist and xenophobic and sexist ideologies. They were fine with his trans-phobia, anti-Semitism and Islamophobia. They were fine with how he encourages his followers to harass women and people of color and transgender people online. . . . Certainly, Simon & Schuster was not alone in what they were willing to tolerate. A great many people were perfectly comfortable with the tar-gets of Milo's hateful attention until that attention hit too close to home.

This is the dirty secret about freedom of speech; rather than being an ideal, it is a litmus test of a society's prejudices. Milo's case proves that, very bluntly, many saw the harassment of women and people of color as inoffensive, or at least as an opinion that can be tolerated and, where his publisher was concerned, an opinion that could be sold. When Gay says the red line was breached when it "hit too close to home," this is not just a turn of phrase. "Home" in this scenario is anything that the powerful forces in a society consider to be their own. The sexual exploitation of children is something any-one can abhor, but other races, religions, sexual orientations are just that—"other," not "home"—and so are fair game. That is the honest appraisal of why people like Milo are indulged, and not because of any cant about freedom of speech.

Hypocrisy about free speech is also bolstered by commercial motivations on the part of tech companies that have a financial interest in keeping speech laws as wide and open to interpretation as possible. If a column of mine was published but the thread was not opened, readers would find me on social media and cry censorship, then unleash whatever invective they were prevented from spewing below the line at the *Guardian* on Twitter, or Instagram, or Facebook, which had, shall we say, a much more commercial attitude to moderation. The company's duty of care was to its bottom line. As platforms multiplied, there were more and more ways for me to receive feedback from readers. I could be sworn at and told to go back to where I came from via at least three platforms. The comment thread seemed redundant. The whole internet was now a comment thread, but with moderators who have the opposite goal to those at the *Guardian*. Social networking moderators delete as little content as possible and suspend as few accounts as possible. The act of limiting posts and users is inimical to the business models of social networks. Vijaya Gadde, Twitter's head of trust and safety, legal and public policy, said in an interview with *Motherboard* that she thinks "there's a fundamental mission that we're serving, our purpose of the company, which is to serve the public conversation." To serve that conversation, Twitter needs to permit "as many people in the world as possible for engaging on a public platform, and it means that we need to be open to as many viewpoints as possible."

That means having a very flexible definition of what violates codes of conduct, allowing abuse and harassment to grow unchecked on the platform. In the last six months of 2018, almost eleven million accounts were reported. Twitter took action on just over 5 percent of those cases. In the United States, tech companies have the right to choose what speech is hosted on their sites because they operate as private businesses. And because speech is the literal product of social media companies, they must ensure that they retain the ability to police it as loosely as possible. Tech companies such as You-

Tube and Google, and social media companies such as Twitter, must also maintain another condition of their ability to allow millions of users to post hateful and abusive content—not being held liable for that content. As a result of these incentives, the definition of free speech as far as powerful tech companies is concerned has to stay as absolute as possible. A lot of money and lobbying goes into that. As questions about the impunity of white supremacists and abusive trolls online have become more frequent over the past decade, Twitter's lobbying spend in Washington has increased. By 2020, Twitter was spending more in the first three months of the year than it had in all of 2014. In 2019, the company spent its highest lobbying outlay in the history of the firm at just under $1.5 million. Other tech companies were doing the same. In the same year, Facebook's lobbying spend was $16.7 million. When a woman is targeted by a violent partner or anonymous stalker online, she is up against this kind of power and capital. To tech companies, victims like her are just the cost of doing business.

This expansion of online speech became a tail that wagged the dog of traditional media outlets. All the heat, the controversy, and the drama was online. And with vastly expanded parameters of acceptable speech, real-life media began to adopt the same standards, fishing in social media pools for debates and arguments. The glut of opinion inevitably meant that as less and less speech was out of bounds, public discussions also treated all positions as valid, all opinions as worthy of airing as long as there was an opposing one.

I began to see this false equivalence in my own media engagements. I would be called upon by more neutral outlets, such as the BBC, to discuss increasingly absurd arguments with other journalists or political activists with extreme views. Conversations around race, immigration, Islam, and climate change became more binary and polarized when there were no binaries to be contemplated. Climate change deniers were allowed to broadcast falsehoods about a reversal in climate change. Racial minorities were called upon to counter thinly veiled racist or xenophobic views. I found myself, along with other journalists in the media industry, regularly ambushed. Appearing on BBC's *Newsnight* to discuss an incident where a far-right racist had mounted a mosque pavement with his car and killed one of the congregation, and after I tried to make the point that there was insufficient focus on a growing far-right terror threat, the interviewer asked me: "Have you had abuse? Give us an example." This became a frequent line of inquiry, the personalization and provocation of personal debate when what was needed was analysis.

It became common for me and like-minded colleagues to query, when invited on the TV or radio to discuss such topics as immigration or Islamophobia, who was appearing on the other side, because the interlocutors were increasingly just garden-variety racists dressed up with the titles of columnists or authors. This is now the discourse; presenting bigotry and then the defense of bigotry as a "debate" from which everyone can benefit, like a boxing match where even the loser is paid along with the promoters, coaches, and whole cast behind arranging the fight. The writer Reni Eddo-Lodge has called it "performing rage."

Views that had previously been consigned to the political fringes made their way into the mainstream via social and traditional media organizations that previously would never have contemplated their airing. The expansion of media outlets meant that it was not only marginalized voices that secured access to the public, but also those with more extreme and fringe views. These characters began to punch above their weight in the marketplace of ideas; all they needed was an internet connection. And they realized very early on that there was a loophole; slap "free speech" on offensive, inciteful, and untruthful proclamations, and people will think twice before shutting you down.

In my own journalism, it became clear that whenever I attempted to push back against what amounted to incitement of a crime against racial or religious minorities, opponents fixated on the free speech argument, rather than the harmful ramifications of hate speech.

My pushback was not intolerance of speech. It was simply more speech—speech objecting to racist and sexist statements. And because the influx from the extremes has brought more objectionable speech, more opposition to it has been raised. Believers in the free speech crisis myth see this pushback as intolerance and misread it as a change in free speech attitudes.

Not only do free speech warriors demand all opinions be heard on all platforms they choose, whether it be college campuses or Twitter, they demand that there be no objection or reaction. This argument is psychologically taxing for anyone who can see the dangers of hate speech and the connection between a sharpening tenor on immigration, for example, and how this could be used to make the lives of immigrants and minorities harder. It is, according to the director of the UK-based Institute of Race Relations, Liz Fekete, "the privileging of freedom of speech over freedom to life."

Free speech crisis advocates always seem to have an agenda. They overwhelmingly want to exercise their freedom of speech to agitate against minorities, women, immigrants, and Muslims. But they dress these base impulses up in the language of concern or anti-establishment conspiracy. Similar to the triggers of political correct-ness hysteria, there is a direct correlation between the rise in free speech panic and the rise in far-right or hard-right political energy, as evidenced by anti-immigration, right-wing electoral successes in the US, the UK, and across continental Europe. As the space for these views expanded, so the concept of free speech became frayed and tattered. It began to mean many things, to lose its grounding caveats, caught between fact and opinion, between action and reac-tion. The discourse became mired in a misunderstanding of free speech as absolute.

The oligarchy of ideas

The first question when any freedom of speech issue comes up shouldn't be about whether speech is being restricted, it should be about who has the most power. Is it the speaker, or the spoken about? Milo was indulged because trolling has become an industry, but he was also indulged because those he attacked did not have enough power. The skew of power elevates certain speakers based not on the merit of their ideas, but on their commercial value. Political dis-course is now a sort of lucrative contact sport where insults and lies are hurled on television, radio, online outlets, and in the press, and audiences pay to heckle and cheer. CNN's coverage of the "Trump transition," after Donald Trump was elected as US president, was a modern version of a medieval circus. Step right up and gawk at Richard Spencer, the Trump supporter and head of far-right think tank the National Policy Institute, as he questions whether Jews "are people at all, or instead soulless golem." See the black Trump surro-gate who thinks Hillary Clinton started the war in Syria. And here's

Corey Lewandowski, a man who appeared on CNN as a political commentator, but who appears to make a living from lying in the media. Yes, he's the one who alleged that Trump's birther story, his version of the claim that Barack Obama was not born on US soil, was in fact started by Hillary Clinton. In pursuit of ratings—from behind a "freedom of speech" fig leaf and perhaps the good intention of balance on the part of some—many media platforms have detoxified radical and untruthful behavior that was until recently confined to the darker corners of Reddit and Breitbart. That radical and untruthful behavior has a direct impact on how safe the world is for those smeared by these performances. Trump himself was the main act in this lucrative show. Initially seen as an entertaining side act during his election campaign, his offensive, untruthful, and pugnacious online presence became instantly more threatening and dangerous once he was elected. Inevitably, his verbal and written incontinence, his bitterness, rage, and hate-mongering, by sheer dint of constant exposure, became less and less shocking and, in turn, less and less extreme.

A world where all opinions and lies are presented to the public as a sort of take-it-or-leave-it buffet is often described as the *marketplace of ideas*, a rationalization for freedom of expression based on comparing ideas to products in a free market economy. The marketplace of ideas model of free speech holds that what is true factually, and what is good morally, will emerge after a competition of ideas in a free, unmoderated, and transparent public discourse—a healthy debate where the truth will prevail. Bad ideas and ideologies will lose out and wither away when they are vanquished by superior ones. The problem with the marketplace of ideas theory (as with all "invisible hand" theories) is that it doesn't account for a world in which the market is skewed and not all ideas receive equal representation, because the market has monopolies and cartels.

The inherent imbalances in the American media summarized in Chapter 1 render it less a marketplace of ideas and more a sort of prison store or commissary that provides few and overpriced goods to captive consumers. And the concept of the market that we are aspiring to in our speech laws actually requires a lot of regulation. There are anti-monopoly rules, there are interest rate fixes and, in many markets, artificial currency pegs. In the press, publishing, and the business of idea dissemination in general, there are players who are deeply entrenched and networked, and so the supply of ideas reflects their power.

In a world where funding and lobbying groups can sponsor public opinion makers from university all the way through to publication of their first book, where lazy or time-stressed TV producers keep returning to the same voices for their commentary, and where publishers and top media executives tend to come broadly from the same pool, social class, and universities, it is inevitable that there is a failure of curation. This is not deliberate. There is no actual oligarchy ruling from a glass tower and conspiring to keep other voices out, but there is a cumulative imbalance, an uneven ground which means freedom of speech becomes concentrated in a few stables. Even though there are more platforms and little regulation of speech on those platforms, the views that are projected are still those of an influential minority.

Claims about the free speech crisis entirely omit the element of power. We are told that power lies with some abstract "mob" of marginalized identities and their smooth-tongued allies. But where does the real power lie? Who gets to make legislation about speech? Who gets to enforce it? Who gets to benefit from it and who has the profile and the platforms to wield it? A general rule of thumb when you are trying to figure out who has the power in any given free speech situation is to identify which party is most vocal about being silenced. Chances are, they have the most power. The media landscape is so skewed that those you can hear complaining about being silenced are, by definition, those who have the access to enough platforms to make that noise. What they are really saying is *My views, which I am expressing here, are not as universally accepted as they were before, and that's just not good enough.*

Lacking the finesse of the usual free speech hypocrites, Donald Trump's Twitter account has exposed their endgame. He spent years in office breaking almost every Twitter rule on abuse, spreading misinformation, and inciting violence, yet he was only banned when he had definitely lost the presidency. He has two things that social media platforms cannot dismiss—power and commercial value. When the world's media rushes to cover a powerful person's words on Twitter, that has a direct impact on Twitter's share price and financial future. After a few tense years of Trump making a mockery of Twitter's violation policy, he finally tweeted something even Twitter couldn't ignore. When Minneapolis erupted in protests after the police murder of George Floyd, an African American man whose life ebbed away under the knee of a white police officer, Trump tweeted:

These THUGS are dishonoring the memory of George Floyd, and I won't let that happen. Just spoke to Governor Tim Walz and told him that the Military is with him all the way. Any dif-

ficulty and we will assume control but, when the looting starts,
the shooting starts. Thank you!

Twitter slapped a notice on the tweet saying it "violated the Twitter rules about glorifying violence. However, Twitter has determined that it may be in the public's interest for the tweet to remain accessible." Two tweets that Trump had posted two days prior had been fact-checked by Twitter. Trying to find a delicate way of saying the tweets were lies so as not to trigger a man who had the ability to mobilize regulators against the company, Twitter labeled them as "potentially misleading."

There really is no clearer example of how free speech is a right that is subject almost entirely to controls unrelated to the actual content of speech. Trump violated the rules, and Twitter let him do it because a variety of factors exempted him. But what was a blatant pass infuriated Trump. He accused Twitter of "interfering" in the 2020 presidential election and "stifling" free speech. In the name of that free speech, in his indignation that any form of judgment should be passed on his exhortation of violence, Trump issued an executive order. The purpose of the order was to expose Twitter to legal liability for its users' content. Before he issued the order, Trump warned (on Twitter) that, if the company continued to "silence conservative voices," Republicans would move to "strongly regulate" social media companies or "close them down." Trump essentially threatened to use his power to remove this protection, to retaliate against Twitter for the (extremely soft) labels appended to his tweets. More chillingly though, he used his power to intimidate Twitter into letting him post falsehoods and glorification of violence against minorities.

This directly violated the First Amendment. Official punishment for protected speech, according to the Supreme Court, "offends the Constitution." On these grounds, a lawsuit was filed by the Center for Democracy and Technology (CDT) and it called Trump's order "retaliatory" because it specifically attacked Twitter for using its First Amendment right to comment and moderate the president's tweets. Trump invoked free speech so that he could violate it.

This, in a nutshell, is what free crisis mythology achieves. Taken to its natural conclusion, the myth of the free speech crisis enables the powerful to leverage their considerable resources against the weak. In doing so they create a two-tier system. On the top sit those with access to platforms and the ability to regulate these platforms or enrich them. Think of them as the free speech wealthy, accumulating and hoarding speech capital. They then use that capital to squash any challenge arising from the lower tier, in which sit groups who have a fraction of the visibility and resources. Those who really have the power to limit speech use freedom of expression to impose their definition of what constitutes free speech. When free speech crisis events are faked, the platforms, be they Twitter or the *New York Times*, are pronounced unfit to manage their free speech responsibilities, and so the right is taken away from them. Like all myth pushers, what the speech warriors decry isn't the limiting of freedoms, it's the limiting of freedoms by those other than themselves.

The entitlement to free speech impunity is also a tactic. Claiming to be silenced plays an important part in both sexing up views that have become dulled by mainstreaming while at the same time conferring a sort of underdog legitimacy on plain old bigotry. But what happens when there is no evidence that prejudice is being silenced by a cabal of liberals? Well, then it must be fabricated.

Fabrication—Free Speech Grifting and No-Platforming

Characters who have successfully monetized free-speech controversy trade in a sort of insurance-scam politics, where an individual throws themselves at a sensitive area and then claims they are victimized by political correctness, by the left, or by women—or by all of the above—before cashing in on the attention. An example of this is Milo threatening to name undocumented students from his speaker's podium at Berkeley and getting exactly the response he might have hoped for. Protestors prompted police to evacuate him before he could even speak. If there were no internet most lightning rods and their attendant free speech controversies would not exist. Milo refers to himself as an "internet supervillain."

The calibration of free speech in a digital context is something we have not even begun to grapple with, choosing still to litigate it as if it were simply a matter of competing views. There have been moves to ban or demonetize the social media accounts of people who have made free speech a commercial success. Milo himself was banned from Twitter after it embarked on a flushing out of white supremacists. But these measures are random, inchoate, and are not linked to any solid policy on hate speech and smaller, less high-profile users continue the work of the banned marquee names. The companies that host such self-styled internet villains have competing interests, and so it's extremely hard to make responsible calls on the harm these characters are inflicting. They have to balance their bottom line—one which is fed by the traffic that abuse and hate speech create—with their responsibilities as platform providers. Twitter, in particular, demonstrates the mess that is online free speech policy. Abuse on the platform is ubiquitous and reluctantly policed because to block every vile user is either prohibitive or at some point harms the business model, which is built on user growth. And so, the internet supervillains thrive.

The writer Mari Uyehara calls this group "Free Speech Grifters." They come from a broad church, one that encompasses cynical bottom-feeders such as Milo and various other digital con artists, but also a more rarefied bunch—the pin-striped grifters, who use free speech as a tool to score points against progressive causes. These are gentrified, suited, slick operators such as Bill Maher, a popular HBO talk-show host whose show *Real Time with Bill Maher* has been running for seventeen years. Maher, who has called Islam "the motherlode of bad ideas" and suggested that "if Muslim men could get laid more, we wouldn't have this problem," dedicates far more time alleging that he is persecuted for criticizing Islam than he does addressing an epidemic of Islamophobia in which he is an active and vocal participant. "Either I say exactly what you want me to say, or else I am a bigot," he moaned when called out over demeaning comments about Islam. When objections were raised to him giving a commencement speech at Berkeley, he said that people wanted him disinvited because "I'm a racist. Right, because Islam is a race."

"Given the myopic focus on liberals," Uyehara pointed out in *GQ* magazine, "it would seem that Free Speech Grifters are not actually interested in the free exchange of ideas, per se; they are interested in liberal caricature for clicks, social-media followings, and monetization." They are interested in goading people into performing rage, so that rage can be recycled as censoriousness, which in turn enhances their stature as liberal inquisition martyrs. *Grifting* fabricates free speech crisis news and events, the same way the grievance industry fabricates PC crisis reports. The final stage is where the scam really pays off, in that with every alleged silencing incident, the censored views receive even more attention.

Much of free speech moral panic stems from incidents of no-platforming. The 2018 bestseller *The Coddling of the American Mind* claims that there is a crisis of "safetyism" among the young precipitated by observing the language of microaggressions, the tribalism of identity politics and intersectionality. These arguments are an updating of similar ones made as far back as the early '90s in such books—also best sellers—as Dinesh D'Souza's *Illiberal Education*. The American right and center are so fixated with the academy that the manipulation of data to come up with campus free speech hysteria headlines is a common practice. Research by Georgetown University's Free Speech Project published in 2018 takes issue with what has become an entire genre of free speech panic on US campuses, one that includes books and online magazines and is the theme of regular columns in the American press. The research looked at both alleged incidents of free speech violations on campus and at the overall trends regarding freedom of expression among college students in particular, and liberals in general. The conclusion was that overall public support for free speech has in fact risen over time, not fallen, and that those on the political right are less supportive of free speech than those on the left. The research also concluded that college graduates are on the whole more supportive of speech than non-graduates and that college students are less likely than the overall population to support restrictions on speech on campus.

The academic Jeffrey Sachs came to the same conclusion after sifting through data on attitudes among US college students toward freedom of speech, and on incidents of free speech terminations or withdrawal of platforms based on political ideology. The most compelling data comes from a "disinvitation database" created by the Foundation for Individual Rights in Education (FIRE), a watchdog group that promotes free expression on campuses and tracks attempts by students to disinvite or prevent campus speakers. It showed just thirty-five attempts at disinvitation in 2017, down from forty-three in 2016. Sachs makes the point that out of a pool of almost five thousand colleges, disinvitation attempts—and by extension attempts that have actually succeeded—are quite rare. According to FIRE, in 2018, there were nine attempts at disinvitation. Among them was the political commentator Dave Rubin, invited to debate at the University of New Hampshire. His invitation was opposed for racial and anti-immigration views that the student body found objectionable. The opposition was not successful.

"There is no campus free speech crisis," Sachs concluded. "The right's new moral panic is largely imaginary."

There are also indications that insurance-scam politics are at play here. In the United States, well-funded right-wing groups are increasingly funneling controversial speakers onto campuses, in some instances paying and training them, with the purpose of provoking a protest that can then be used as evidence of left-wing campus illiberalism. In 2017, SUNY Buffalo hosted Robert Spencer, an anti-Muslim author and blogger who was quoted sixty-four times in the manifesto of Norwegian mass-murderer Anders Breivik and by other Western writers who shared his view that Muslim immigrants pose a grave danger to Western culture. This was not an invitation that arose organically out of the normal course of events at the college. He was invited by the Young America's Foundation, a well-funded conservative lobbying group that engages in gotcha tactics to promote its right-wing culture wins. On social media, the organization's tone is pugilistic and seems less concerned with promoting conservative values than it is with scoring points against the left and "triggering the libs." In 2018, it promoted videos and content with captions such as: "💥 SHOTS FIRED 💥 @DLoesch completely EXPOSES the Left's gun control agenda! You can't fool her" and "👏 THERE 👏 ARE 👏 ONLY 👏 TWO 👏 GENDERS 👏 WHEN WILL THE LEFT LEARN??? @BenShapiro has had enough."

The foundation paid Robert Spencer a $2,000 fee and trained a student leader to organize both the event and the distribution of literature beforehand. They then waited for the money shot. And they got it. Members of the college's Muslim population and non-Muslim sympathizers staged a sit-in, although Spencer's talk was allowed to proceed. Inevitably the headline became about the protest, something that Spencer himself appeared to be briefed on, as he concluded his talk by saying: "The forces you are enabling are going to come back to haunt you."

On the group's website, it boasted of "dispatching" thirty-one speakers to colleges in one month in 2017. Among them was Ann Coulter. After Spencer's talk, the *New York Times* reported on this new tactic of using speakers to create free speech crisis controversies. The report pointed out that the foundation's invitees seemed to be getting edgier and more controversial. The report gave voice to protestors who questioned "whether such events are cynically intended to provoke reactions." A student quoted by the paper said that regular speaker controversies were "part of a larger systematic and extremely well-funded effort to disrupt public universities and create tension among student groups on campus."

It is often the case, when following the breadcrumbs of a myth, to find that not only is it not true, but that its *opposite* is true. At the biggest campus protest against Robert Spencer, at Stanford University in 2017, more than four hundred students, including Muslims and their allies, held a rally objecting to his talk. Spencer's event went ahead with little disruption. Despite the fact that Spencer prevailed in the face of alleged silencing from Muslims he was smearing, he still dedicated his speech to "the most marginalized community at Stanford University, the College Republicans"—which drew a titter from his audience. What research did find, was that even though data indicates a trend toward more willingness to hear from disagreeable people, the exception to that was speech from disagreeable Muslims. In 2008, NORC's General Social Survey research created a hypothetical Muslim clergyman who preaches against America and asked people if he should be allowed to teach at a college. Two thirds of American responders believed he should not. *Vox* also found that the perception of Muslims as quick to take offense was not correct. When the website published controversial cartoons depicting the prophet Mohammed, it received no complaints. For covering Islamophobia, *Vox* received dozens.

Not only does the data show that there is no free speech crisis as such, it also illustrates that, as myths tend to do, there is a mobilization against progressive causes that outstrips any activity on the allegedly censorious left. An analysis of the FIRE disinvitation data by Heterodox Academy shows that the most successful attempts to shut down speakers have come from right-leaning groups. The analysis concluded that "speaker disinvitation attempts have a higher success rate when they come from the right of the speaker (54.64 percent) than when they come from the left of the speaker (32.89 percent)."

All these conclusions do not seem to be making a dent in the overall conventional wisdom about a freedom of speech crisis. And attention is being diverted from what is essentially a growing resistance movement. There was only one type of speech that Jeffrey Sachs found to be tolerated less—racist speech. "On issue after issue," Sachs tweeted, "young people aged 18–34 are the MOST tolerant of potentially offensive speech *and trending upward*, while older Americans are the least." There was "one important exception," he stated, "tolerance for racist speech, where the age relationship is reversed." I spoke to him a few weeks after he published this research. He mentioned that what is often missed when discussing free speech crisis mythology is the degree of polarization that is present in these debates.

The increasing intolerance of racist speech and the increasing scale of racist provocations are intersecting lines and we are drawing the wrong conclusion—that there is a free speech crisis. In fact, there is a power crisis and its effect is the quieting of voices that are protesting harmful speech. Free speech proponents dismiss this objection to harmful speech and delegitimize it by calling it a rejection of free speech. They deploy "what next" fallacies and claim that curbing free speech, even if that speech is harmful, is a slippery slope.

The Tool—The Slippery Slope

The logic of the "slippery slope" is the technical tool that the freedom of speech crisis myth deploys to either end the argument or divert attention away from the inconvenient distinctions and nuances that conflate freedom of speech and the "right to platform" with freedom from consequence. It goes something like this: if you silence views you do not like, then you will be silenced next. University of Amsterdam academic Magdalena Jozwiak summarizes the slippery slope argument as: "Today this speech restriction, tomorrow the Inquisition."

It is a compelling argument that has achieved almost canonical status. It just sounds like it makes sense. It seems neat and logical and the imagery, that of an evil nourished by our shortsightedness, is vivid. Its essence is in theologian Martin Niemöller's famous confessional, "First they came . . . ," which ends with the chilling line, "Then they came for me—and there was no one left to speak for me."

It is also a flattering conviction. To believe in defending views with which you disagree implies a moral robustness and intellectual largesse. But the slippery slope argument is based on false equivalence. Indeed, censoring Nazis might actually *prevent* the next holocaust. There is simply no evidence that the slippery slope exists.

On an abstract level, slippery slope logic only holds if the initial premise is plausible. But is incendiary, demeaning, threatening, or stigmatizing speech equivalent to all other possible forms of speech? It is less "First they came for the socialists, and I did nothing, then they came for me," and more "First they came for the Holocaust deniers, and then they did not come for me or anyone else, because none of us were Holocaust deniers."

In a 2015 paper entitled "Internet, Freedom of Speech and Slippery Slope Argument—The Case of the 'Right to Be Forgotten,'" Jozwiak wrote that "slippery slope arguments are however slippery themselves: if any limits of freedom of speech are simply too dangerous to be accepted, why not call for tearing down the copyrights, or law prohibiting deceptive commercial speech?"

Another version of the slippery slope fallacy is "where do you draw the line?" For example, if neo-Nazi groups are restricted, then might other unpopular Nazi groups also be silenced on the basis that they are advancing some sort of racially divisive idea? And if they're banned, then the next adjacent group will be banned, and so on. "Where do you draw the line?"

Well, you draw it in the same place as myriad other lines drawn by society's customary and legal boundaries. The line-drawing fallacy argues that just because a precise line cannot be drawn between two things, no other distinctions can be made. It is a binary argument that suggests "this is the beginning of the end." All the time.

Policing hate is not always very straightforward, sometimes lines might get blurred and mistakes may even be made, but on the whole, it should be possible to make the distinction between hate speech and other kinds of speech.

The "Next the inquisition" argument is popular because it appeals to both the right and the left. The right dislikes any regulation, and the "what next?" bogeyman is useful in limiting any bans or restrictions. The left shares this reluctance to control speech because of progressive positions on individual liberty and right to express dissent. The origin of free speech advocacy is in antiauthoritarianism; it is intended to protect the right to oppose and criticize power, be it the Church or the secular state, without fear of punishment. The left continued this tradition by trying to maintain the widest possible definition of protected speech. In the United States, the three seminal Supreme Court decisions on free speech in the twentieth century were successfully brought by the left in order to prevent a chilling of dissent. The decisions made for a higher burden of proof to show "clear and present danger" before blocking speech, the allowance for false statements of fact when criticizing public officials, and the objection to "prior restraints" such as injunctions and licensing laws to forbid speech. It is difficult for some on the left to come to terms with the fact that free speech principles are now being used by the powerful to attack the weak. And so, left-wingers argue technicalities, while those they set out to protect, the dissenters, the vulnerable and excluded, are savaged.

Freedom to respond

Freedom of speech is not a neutral, fixed concept, uncolored by societal prejudice. The belief that it is some absolute untainted hallmark of civilization is linked to self-serving exceptionalism, a delusion that there is a basic template around which there is a consensus uninformed by biases. The recent history of fighting for freedom of speech has gone from noble, striving for the right to publish works that offend people's sexual or religious prudery and speaking up against the values leveraged by the powerful to maintain control, to attacking the weak and persecuted. The effort has evolved from challenging upward to punching downward.

The myth of the free speech crisis has been pushed by right-wing funding and activism, but it has also been indulged by liberals who are prone to commitment to abstract ideals that are virtuous in essence but sometimes unfit for application without modulation. Enlightenment prophets and their aphorisms are rolled out, but with little accounting for nuance or adjustment for a modern context—it is no wonder that the US Constitution, extended from Enlightenment values, is often critiqued as fossilized. The quote often misattributed to Voltaire—"I disapprove of what you say, but I will defend to the death your right to say it"—is thrown like a single blanket over a house fire.

The truth is that freedom of speech, even to some of its most passionate founding philosophers, always comes with brake mechanisms, and those mechanisms usually reflect cultural bias. John Milton advocated the destruction of works that are blasphemous or libelous: "Those which otherwise come forth, if they be found mischievous and libelous, the fire and the executioner will be the timeliest and the most effectual remedy, that mans [*sic*] prevention can use." Today, our brake mechanisms include laws against libel, slander, and prejudicing of ongoing legal cases. But these mechanisms do not curb the promotion of hate toward those at the bottom end of the social hierarchy because their protection is not truly a valued and integral part of our popular culture.

Judith Butler, a cultural theorist and Berkeley professor, speaking at a 2017 forum sponsored by the Berkeley Academic Senate, said: "If free speech does take precedence over every other constitutional principle and every other community principle, then perhaps we should no longer claim to be weighing or balancing competing principles or values. We should perhaps frankly admit that we have agreed in advance to have our community sundered, racial and sexual minorities demeaned, the dignity of trans people denied, that we are, in effect, willing to be wrecked by this principle of free speech."

A moral right to express unpopular opinions is not a moral right to express those opinions in a way that silences the voices of others or puts them in danger of violence. What is at stake in challenging free speech crisis mythology is not the resolution of some esoteric argument. Speech has real-life effects. It corrodes community relations, picks on the vulnerable, and threatens the safety of our fellow citizens. By fixating on the free speech element, we have put sanctity of expression over sanctity of life.

The Myth of Harmful Identity Politics

> It means: this man should not be treated as a ter-
> rorist. It means: we have found and isolated the
> problem. Most importantly it means: you are
> safe. He was alone. There is no one else.
>
> —*Amelia Tait on the white male terrorist as "lone wolf"*

On the evening of May 25, 2020, George Floyd, an African American resident of Minneapolis, bought a packet of cigarettes from a grocery store. One of the grocery store employees suspected that the twenty-dollar bill used by Floyd was counterfeit. He asked Floyd, who had recently lost his job due to the coronavirus epidemic, to give the cigarettes back. Floyd was a regular at the store, and according to the owner, a familiar, friendly, and pleasant customer. But the owner of the store was not in that day, leaving a teenage male employee in charge. So, when Floyd refused to give him the cigarettes back, the employee called the police.

Seven minutes after the call, two police officers arrived. Floyd had not fled the scene. He was still there, sitting in a car. One of the police officers drew his gun and ordered Floyd to show his hands.

Once handcuffed, a scuffle ensued when Floyd expressed anxiety about being put in the back of the police car. Policeman Derek Chauvin arrived on the scene, and while Floyd was on the ground, put his knee on Floyd's neck. It was then that several bystanders began filming. Floyd began pleading. He couldn't breathe. "You're killing me," he said at one point. He pleaded for just over six minutes, after which he fell silent. Chauvin still did not budge. Onlookers, who had noticed that Floyd had stopped moving, urged the policeman to check his pulse. There was none. He was pronounced dead one hour later. Chauvin had his knee on Floyd's neck for seven minutes and forty-six seconds. For the last three of those minutes, Floyd was still. The whole episode that ended in Floyd's death took a half hour.

Chauvin was fired and later charged with third degree murder after a national spasm of rage hurried proceedings along. Without the cell phone footage of the death, it is difficult to say with certainty that justice would have been met. During his years of service, Chauvin had been involved in multiple shootings of non-white victims, the subject of twenty complaints and two letters of reprimand.

Police violence in America against people of color is a daily jeopardy. It is a random and constant threat that exists mainly because white perpetrators get away with it. Previous protest or riot has made only a dent in the amnesty white law enforcement officers enjoy, and so there is no incentive to change, especially when there is no one filming. Held hostage on this civilian level, American minorities also face another offensive, this one militarized and coordinated. This other movement is a white, orchestrated terrorism that has claimed more lives than any other terrorist movement since 9/11.

But somehow, the idea of a widely practiced white identity politics which is hostile and aggressive is not an established part of the modern political discourse. Even when white identity politics is manifested in coordinated violent acts its threat is minimized as the work of lone wolves and bad apples. A strange oversight, considering that exclusionary white identity politics has been a cornerstone of domestic and overseas American politics for the last two centuries. Other identity-based political movements such as the Black Lives Matter movement ask merely for equal treatment, yet they are swiftly defined as identity-driven and are roundly condemned and pathologized.

This double standard is applied to all political activity that is based on racial identity. There is a lacuna, a color blindness so to speak, to acts of politics committed by white people, or in the name of whiteness, as compared to those committed in reaction to the wielding of that white power. This is the myth of harmful identity politics: that group behavior to secure rights denied on racial grounds is corrosive, restricted to non-majority white groups, and is offensive, rather than defensive.

The harmful identity politics myth creates an *exception for whiteness*, promotes racial entitlement via dog whistling—*the wink*—and *grievance flipping*, and is sustained by appeals to *universalism*. Constant denial that race is relevant to how white populations behave politically helps prop up the myth that only other races are motivated by identity. This denial minimizes the menace of white race-based animus: it's just "white self-interest," or a number of other euphemisms.

For the purposes of this chapter, there are two definitions of identity politics. The first is the effort to secure the rights denied to some on the basis of their identity—defensive identity politics.

The second is that which seeks domination on the basis of identity—aggressive identity politics. This chapter will focus on identity politics along ethnic or racial lines and the different standards and definitions applied in order to render white identity politics natural and benign, and identity politics as practiced by others as dangerous. But it's only due to absence of space that I cannot flesh out all the other ways "default" identities, those vested with so much power that they do not see themselves as identities at all—maleness, heterosexuality, heteronormativity—also conspire to dismiss the concerns of others marginal to them.

An Exception for Whiteness

There is a discount applied to behavior by those we see as our own. In Saudi Arabia, it was official policy never to use the word "terrorist" or "terrorism" when referring to religious insurgents waging war against the royal family for the past forty years. Perpetrators were referred to as "those who have lost their path," or "the lost ones." Terrorist groups came to be known as "The Lost Front" or "The Lost Category." The purpose of these euphemisms is to avoid othering these individuals and keep the door open to their rehabilitation. In the 1990s, the country even set up a Betty Ford–style deradicalization clinic, offering amnesty once its graduates had completed a full terror detox program. When that was unsuccessful, the Saudi government decided to claim that any internal opposition to it was funded and stoked by external enemies such as Iran and Qatar. Calling Saudis terrorists would imply that not all was well within Saudi society, and that was a truth that Saudi authorities did not want to acknowledge.

White people extend this amnesty to other white people who continue to behave and vote along racial lines harmful to minorities, while condemning other political movements that are based on identity as self-indulgent and detrimental to the achievement of universal goals. The left seeks anti-capitalist goals: healthcare, housing, and unionization. The right's universal goals mostly involve community and national cohesion. These goals cannot be achieved if everyone is competing in the "oppression Olympics."

But the goals for the first declared movement based on identity politics were always universal. In the mid-1970s, a group of Afrocentric black feminist scholars and activists in the United States formed an organization specifically to address the concerns of black women, concerns which they felt had been ignored by the wider feminist movement. They called themselves the Combahee River Collective, the name of the location from which the abolitionist Harriet Tubman launched a military campaign in 1863 to successfully liberate more than 750 slaves.

In 1977, the group released "A Black Feminist Statement," in which they declared that they were "actively committed to struggling against racial, sexual, heterosexual, and class oppression" and that black feminism was "the logical political movement to combat the manifold and simultaneous oppressions that all women of color face." They concluded that other groups were not up to the task of helping black women and people of color in general, and that it was therefore incumbent upon the collective to advance independently. "We realize that the only people who care enough about us to work consistently for our liberation are us. . . . This focusing on our own oppression is embodied in the concept of identity politics. We believe that the most profound and potentially the most radical politics come directly out of our own identity, as opposed to working to end somebody else's oppression."

If one ended the reading there, it would indeed appear that this was a splinter group, a balkanization of resistance. And most analyses do end there. But if we read on, the statement goes on to say: "If Black women were free, it would mean that everyone else would have to be free since our freedom would necessitate the destruction of all the systems of oppression." These black women were not splitting off from a main movement, they were establishing an infantry in a defensive coalition of oppressed peoples where a common purpose is achieved via the pursuit of a specific group goal.

Critics see defensive identity politics as a disruptive influence that divides the electorate. Implicit in this critique is some notion that the group seeking change is being disruptive for no reason—and the rational reaction to this kind of violent disruption is to support a law-and-order or populist candidate. But defensive identity politics is in fact a reflexive movement that is responding to both the constant subordination of the non-mainstream identity and the recent, aggressive pushback against equality. It is a response against the dominance and ubiquity of a white identity. As Hannah Arendt wrote: "If one is attacked as a Jew, one must defend oneself as a Jew." When you are attacked and threatened because of your identity, you respond in terms of your identity. When the Republican gubernatorial candidate Roy Moore ran his 2017 campaign, his history of racist positions came to light. This was a candidate who said that America was better during the slavery era, that the Quran was comparable to Hitler's *Mein Kampf*, and who endorsed Trump's animation of the Obama birther conspiracy. Black voters turned out and voted against him in their racial interest, regardless of ideology. When they were threatened as blacks, they voted in one racial bloc.

Crucial to the pathologizing of non-white identity politics is the belief that whiteness is the default. So much of mythology is due to this defaulting of certain identities—being white, a certain sort of masculine, hailing from a certain class, and being a specific form of straight—as base case, neutral, unmotivated by anything as vulgar as color or gender. The assumption that these identities are simply standard and correct, rather than merely powerful, underpins the need to create myths. These myths then continue to approach resistance to this defaulting as a revolt against the natural order of things, rather than an attempt at correction.

The American political researcher Asad Haider summarized the problem in a 2018 talk: "By coding demands that come from marginal or subordinate groups as identity politics the white male identity is enshrined with the status of the neutral, general and universal." He continued: "We know that this is false, we know that there is a white identity politics, a white nationalism, and in fact whiteness is the prototypical form of racial ideology itself."

The identity politics myth dismisses campaigns for dignity and equal treatment as the work of individuals obsessed with victimhood, and it excuses and even justifies "backlash" political behavior—such as whites across classes voting for Trump in the election. The myth denies victimhood to the subjugated and then blames them for the bad behavior of their oppressors; women are trying to get more than they deserve or have rightfully earned, the victims of hate speech are in fact the intolerant party, those who ask for respect and accommodation of difference are using political correctness to bully others.

In the case of the harmful identity politics myth, this strain is most evolved.

The harmful identity politics myth is based on the belief that things have reverted to some benign mean. Slavery and racial segregation have ended—and for those particularly committed to the myth, they were ended by white people—and so now we must all stop asking for special dispensation. The "politics of recognition" is what the writer Amy Chua calls it because, fundamentally, there are no serious problems anymore that are not universal.

The terminology of exception

Since Trump's election and the Brexit referendum, the euphemisms for votes motivated by racial grievance or anti-immigration sentiment rapidly have become a part of the political lexicon; these people are not racist, they are the "left-behind," acting out because of "economic anxiety." Even when they are not the meek of the earth, they are said to be acting out of "white interest" rather than reinforcing white supremacy. In his book *The Road to Somewhere*, the British journalist and writer David Goodhart adds to the by-another-name lexicon of genteelism with the term "Somewheres," as distinct from "Anywheres." The Somewheres are rooted in a specific place or community, such as a small town or in the countryside. They are socially conservative, less educated, and less mobile than their metropolitan counterparts. The Anywheres are, well, anywhere—unrooted from a particular place or community and able to relocate easily for work, education, or love.

Derek Black, the son of a grand wizard in the Ku Klux Klan (KKK), said in a 2018 NPR interview that "the fundamental belief that drove my dad, drove my parents and my family, over decades . . .

was that race was the defining feature of humanity and that people were only happy if they could live in a society that was only this one biologically defined racial group."

This direct honesty about white racial loyalty is helpful in understanding how minorities, just by existing, are blamed for the bad behavior of white people. Alas, such honesty is rare. Most of the time, critics engage in fine pretzel logic to remain committed to the view that white people behave in a distinct political unit because other identities—merely by existing—absolutely *force* them into it.

In a 2016 op-ed for the *New York Times*, American academic Mark Lilla manages to blame the Trump "whitelash" on liberals, in general, and on Hillary Clinton, in particular. He calls it "identity liberalism." Liberals, he claims, do not recognize "how their own obsession with diversity has encouraged white, rural, religious Americans to think of themselves as a disadvantaged group whose identity is being threatened or ignored." Lilla does not follow that revealing thought with the obvious corollary: that whiteness is, in fact, an identity, and then he goes on to assert: "Liberals should bear in mind that the first identity movement in American politics was the Ku Klux Klan, which still exists. Those who play the identity game should be prepared to lose it." Lilla refuses to acknowledge that non-white identity politics is a necessary and defensive response to that "first identity movement." Populist voters—whether Brexit "Leavers" or Trump's "left-behinders"—are all demonstrating the same thing: aggressive identity politics. The view that defensive identity politics has fractured political solidarity and created white anger fails to account for the fact that whiteness itself is an identity. Not only is it an identity, it is such a clear and potent one that it has consistently erected high barriers to entry via slavery, colonialism, segregation, and institutional discrimination. These barriers created the need for defensive identity politics in the first place.

Racial entitlement

Since 2016, there has been a lot said about "economic anxiety" in the United States and how it motivated white voters to elect Trump. During the campaign, the dust-streaked image of the Appalachian coal miner stalked the pages of the American press. He was losing his living, his extended family support network and community were falling apart, he was alienated and angry. "I kind of feel that people are looking down on us," Neil Hanshew, a miner, told the *New York Times* in August of that year. He was voicing a "common sentiment," the report said. "They're looking at us like we're a bunch of dumb hillbillies who can't do anything else."

The media lapped it up. The *Atlantic* reported that "the billionaire developer is building a blue-collar foundation." The Associated Press pointed out "Trump's success in attracting white, working-class voters." On November 9, 2016, the *New York Times* ran a front-page article saying that Trump's support was "a decisive demonstration of power by a largely overlooked coalition of mostly blue-collar white and working-class voters."

There was a fixation on this most sympathetic of figures. The specter of Hanshew angered the right and shamed the left. But the sympathizers missed two things. There were other disenfranchised working-class voters who didn't flock to Trump. They were not white. And there were affluent people who were not alienated or looked down upon who voted for Trump. The common denominator was not economics, but race. It took about a year for the narrative to catch up.

Research published in the *Washington Post* in late 2017 determined that the economic anxiety claim was, broadly, nonsense. "Contrary to what some have suggested," the authors Matthew Fowler, Vladimir E. Medenica, and Cathy J. Cohen concluded that "white millennial Trump voters were not in more economically precarious situations than non-Trump voters. Fully 86 percent of them reported being employed, a rate similar to non-Trump voters; and they were 14 percent less likely to be low income than white voters who did not support Trump. Employment and income were not significantly related to that sense of white vulnerability. So what was it? Racial resentment."

"White vulnerability" and "racial resentment" are in themselves euphemisms—political correctness is sometimes not a myth, you see, when it comes to refusing to call prejudices what they actually are. Both terms imply that Trump voters' motivation was legitimate and understandable—these people were just vulnerable and resentful. "Racial entitlement" would be a more accurate and less unnecessarily forgiving descriptor. White people who do not want to share the equity they have in society will view demands for more social or economic capital by other racial groups as an encroachment on what rightfully belongs to white people. And so, they vote for candidates who promise them protection of that racial equity. White entitlement is not about economics, it's about status. On the whole, Hillary Clinton lost to Trump among white voters in every single income category, across classes, educations, and incomes. Trump won among poor working-class voters and their wealthy overlords. This was not an economic revolution; it was a white nationalist one.

And those who genuinely felt that they were worse off did so because of racial bias. Feelings of economic anxiety are correlated to racial entitlement. In his book *Post-Racial or Most-Racial? Race and Politics in the Obama Era*, the political scientist Michael Tesler found that perceptions of the American economy were influenced by the color of the president at the time. When Obama was running for reelection in 2012, those voters who registered higher levels of "racial resentment" were less likely to perceive that in reality the unemployment rate, for example, had improved in his first term. Beneficial changes in economic performance did not affect levels of racial resentment. Nor were voters necessarily predisposed to feeling racial grievances when the economy really was doing badly, or when they themselves were worse off. But where Obama was concerned, white voters felt things were worse than they really were no matter the economic reality.

"The evidence is pretty clear," concludes Tesler. "Economic concerns are not driving racial resentment in the Obama Era." It was the other way around. Racial resentment was driving economic anxiety. The *Washington Post* polls found that feelings of entitlement based on race were the single most dependable predictor of "white vulnerability." Everything else, all other variables such as education and economic status, did not make a difference.

This is a situation where false economic analysis is marshaled to legitimize aggressive identity politics. The evidence, both from academic research papers and media polls, that prejudices about race, gender, and immigration animated support for Trump, has been mounting since the election. Trump's tenure was characterized by even more racist and sexist dog whistling, without impacting his popularity among his base. Some called it fear of "losing status" or concerns about "cultural displacement." There were also indications that Trump voters had stronger feelings about the ostensibly declining status of America globally. On the whole, the votes for Trump were not just conservative, they were regressive—in that they were strongly motivated by a need to freeze the status quo, or perhaps by a need to return to the simpler time before Barack Obama's election.

When surveys assessed "social dominance orientation," a psychological measure of a person's belief in hierarchy as necessary and inherent to a society, those who valued hierarchy were more likely to be Trump supporters. They saw in him a protector of their positions. Those positions fell along the lines of race, gender, and culture. In 2018, an author of one such study told the *New York Times* that "it used to be a pretty good deal to be a white, Christian male in America, but things have changed and I think they do feel threatened."

This is not only aggressive identity politics, in the sense that it is political activity along the lines of race, it is paranoia. It is politics that doesn't even have the excuse or justification of grievance. It is an exercise in power maintenance or reclamation rather than an attempt to push back against real injustices. It is shadowboxing.

However, when it comes to white racial entitlement, behavior must clear a very high bar before it is called racist or racially motivated. I was in the United States during the summer of the 2016 election campaign and remember noticing how absent the race question was from the interrogation of Trump voters' motivations. One New York journalist told me—in what became a heated discussion—that coal miners had not mentioned race once when he interviewed them. When he brought up race, they did not seem overly exercised by it. This journalist was absolving his subjects but ignoring the fact that they were not bothered or disturbed by nominee Trump's racist statements about Muslims, Mexicans, and immigrants. He interpreted their ambivalence toward Trump's racism as neutrality, rather than endorsement.

There are broadly two responses when confronted with proof that white people act in racial concert: the first is that it is a reaction to changing demographics and the encroachment of other races—"the browning of America," the demographer William H. Frey called it; the second is that it is benign tribalism—"people preferring their own."

But such responses are nothing new. The dominant identity has been articulating politics in terms of imaginary grievance for as long as there have been minorities demanding anything, from freedom from slavery to freedom from police persecution. While it is non-whites who are accused of overstating their victimhood and triggering that in others, in classic myth fashion, the opposite is true.

In the 1990 US Senate election in Louisiana, David Duke, a former grand wizard of the Ku Klux Klan, ran against incumbent Democratic senator J. Bennett Johnston, and while Johnston was reelected, Duke earned 43 percent of the vote. The justifications for voting for Duke in 1990 are indistinguishable from the reasons white people allegedly voted for Donald Trump in 2016—a working-class, post-recession revolt and an angry message from the disenfranchised to the elites of Washington.

No one seems to ask why this anger can only be expressed by voting for a KKK grand wizard or a man who wants to ban Muslims or build a wall around Mexico, as opposed to, say, Bernie Sanders—a candidate whose main message was one of economic justice. This is the excepting of group white behavior from its obvious animus—racial entitlement—and ascribing benign, even sympathetic, qualities to it.

And the left-behind story is, again, simply not true. Duke picked up the majority of the white vote, and the middle class was split evenly between him and his opponent. He lost only because blacks voted overwhelmingly against him. The same thing happened almost thirty years later with Roy Moore in Alabama. Who can tell those black voters, going to the ballot to vote against a KKK leader and slavery-era nostalgia, that it was not about race and so they should stop playing the identity politics card?

The Wink—It's Not Race

The harmful identity politics myth is sustained by denying that race is an element in white politics while dog whistling that race is, in fact, a central element. *It's not race* is a wink, a secret sign that is flashed at white voters to signify that there are two messages: one for them and one for us. The way to go about it is to absolutely deny in the strongest terms that race has anything to do with a political position, to abhor the very suggestion. It is a trick that has a long and successful history. Even David Duke, a KKK grand wizard—I repeat this point because it bears repeating—was scandalized by the suggestion that race had anything to do with his campaign. Allegations of racism were a "smear," he responded to his supporters. "Remember," he told them at rallies, "when they smear me, they are really smearing you." Nearly three decades later, Steve Bannon, Trump's former strategist, said to a crowd at a French National Front rally in Lille: "Let them call you racists. Let them call you xenophobes. Let them call you nativists. Wear it as a badge of honor." Allegations of racism, according to Bannon, were just bad-faith slurs. For Bannon, white nationalism is patriotism, something which liberals with their "anywhere" unrootedness do not understand.

The language of the wink contains a whole lexicon of terms and postures. One of them is to insist and aggressively deny labels such as "white supremacist" while adopting and promoting white supremacist policies.

Far right and ethno-nationalist groups are very good at the wink. They are very good at dressing up their racism in fancy philosophy and intellectual bluster. The website of the publisher Counter-Currents, for example, describes its mission as one that takes its guiding principles from "French Traditionalist René Guénon's *The Crisis of the Modern World*." Among those principles, as were listed on their website in late 2020, were that we live in a "Dark Age" of intellectual and moral decline, and that knowledge disseminators are essential in guiding humanity out of this stage in its cyclical decline. The publisher, to this aim, publishes works that counter this current. These are all good things; essential ideas, promoting knowledge, resisting the downward trend of intellectual pursuit. Nothing to argue with here. Until you read the works that it publishes, or listen to the podcasts that it produces, and realize that Counter-Currents is in fact a white supremacist organization.

But it's not just any old white supremacist organization. It's one that takes itself very seriously and is aimed at those only with an "IQ over 120." The Southern Poverty Law Center (SPLC) calls Counter-Currents the "epicenter of 'academic' white nationalism." Its editor in chief, Greg Johnson, expends significant energy in distancing its ideology from anything as vulgar as racism. In a way, the more seriously a group or individual takes their racism, the more effort they put into pretending, to the world and even themselves, that there is nothing pejorative here. It's all merely science, merely nature, there is no ill will to any fellow man. The majority of white Identitarians are keen to put as much distance as possible between themselves and the everyday, garden-variety racist, the hooded, cheering, lynch mob participant. They are keen to strip white supremacy from any implication of random violence or cruelty, because these are irrational things, and white supremacy is a rational logical fact. They can look a black person in the eye, they can look at themselves in the mirror, and say, without flinching, that believing in the separation of the races for their own good is not in any way a racist position.

Greg Johnson is the sine qua non for the non-racist racist. His "wink" is to abhor "supremacy" and extol "nationalism." In a Counter-Currents article, he says: "I think that whites are superior to some groups in some ways. I am very proud of our people, and we have a great deal to be proud of. . . . It is easy to find ways in which we are superior to other groups. But you can also find ways in which we are inferior to other groups. I just don't think this issue matters."

Having said that the issue doesn't matter, he goes on to say, in the same article:

> Blacks don't find white civilization comfortable. It is like demanding they wear shoes that are two sizes too small when we impose our standards of punctuality and time preferences, demand that they follow our age-of-consent laws or foist the bourgeois nuclear family upon them. These things don't come naturally to Africans. White standards like walking on the sidewalk, not down the middle of the street, are oppressive to blacks. Such standards are imposed by the hated "white supremacy" system. But if we don't impose white standards upon them, we have chaos. We have great cities like Detroit transformed into wastelands.

The title of the essay from which both these quotes come is "White Nationalists Are Not 'White Supremacists.'"

Racial discord was simply a friction of standards, a culture clash, nothing to do with race. A lot of care goes into such finessing so that racial tension is advanced merely as unfortunate reality rather than an unfair judgment of a race as inferior. It is a particular skill that was honed during the founding years of America, where a belief in its inherent morality, godliness, and exceptionalism had to be reconciled with its savage unholy exploitation and cruelty to black slaves. The *Guardian* writer Gary Younge calls it "the art of deniable racism," where we have plenty of racism "but apparently very few racists."

In order to sustain the moral heart of the American endeavor, white people had to defend slavery not only on economic but also on moral grounds, advancing the theory that slavery was in fact a "positive good" to society. The closer the threat of abolition came, the more hectic and adorned with lofty comparisons this effort became. In order to defend slavery, John C. Calhoun, a political theorist and the seventh vice president of the United States, leaned on Aristotle's theory of natural slavery, the history of Greek democracy, and the glamor and power of the Roman Empire. The argument was that not only was slavery a positive good, it was a feature of successful civilizations.

"Never before has the black race of Central Africa," he said, "from the dawn of history to the present day, attained a condition so civilized and so improved, not only physically, but morally and intellectually. . . . It came to us in a low, degraded, and savage condition, and in the course of a few generations it has grown up under the fostering care of our institutions."

There is a direct line between that early nineteenth-century argument and that in which Greg Johnson sadly observes civilized things "do not come naturally to the African," that the improvement exercise simply did not work.

The embellishing of concepts with historical and philosophical color and the neutralizing of language are pivotal to the wink. The phrase *Make America Great Again*, uniquely supremacist as it seems, is just the latest in a series of such wink phrases that promise restoration of national glory, when what they mean is the preservation of racial hierarchy. It doesn't just play on the right-wing trope that the West has been declining since the emancipation of slaves and women. It also serves as a literal rallying cry.

When I lived under a Sudanese government that used Islamic sharia to purge enemies and justify oppression, I remember how the president and his Islamist party used the phrase "*Allahu Akbar.*" It merely means "God is Great." But it was used to punctuate pugnacious speeches, to celebrate military campaigns, to threaten enemies. It no longer meant "God is Great." It meant "We are Greater." It was intended to foment sectarianism and make a distinction between Us and Them. The "Them" were never specifically named, they were a blank cutout whose features and identity could be painted in. "Make America Great Again" functions exactly the same way. You are greater than—fill in the blank with whoever you feel should be lower than you in status: Mexicans, Muslims, black people.

In a speech in 2016, Bill Clinton pointed out the wink in Make America Great Again. "If you're a white Southerner," Clinton said, "you know exactly what that means, don't you?"

Denying the relevance of race is not just a strategy of white Identitarians or the far right. Politicians deploy it effectively. Congoborn Cécile Kyenge, the first black politician to serve in Italy's government and the first black minister in Italian history, was regularly the target of racist abuse from the country's far-right League Party during her ministerial tenure in 2013–14. She was accused of wanting to impose her "tribal traditions" on Italy and of running a "bonga bonga" government. After an Italian woman was allegedly attacked by an African migrant, a League councillor wrote on Facebook that Kyenge should be raped so she would "know what it feels like." In an interview during which she was shown images of her compared to an orangutan, she called the League Party racist. Four years later, Matteo Salvini, Italy's interior minister and the leader of the League, sued her for defamation. The case is still ongoing.

Donald Trump adopted this denial of racism while hounding people of color. When asked about his history of clear and explicit prejudice, from blocking black tenants from his buildings to fanning the flames of the Obama birther myth, Trump replied that not only was he not racist, he was "the least racist person you have ever met."

The denial works. White, aggressive identity politics is maintained by nailing this implausibility and promoting an agenda of restoring national and racial purity, without making this aim explicit. Such identity politics can only attain mainstream traction by sustaining deniability about fundamentally racist goals. The purpose, the sweet spot of this politics, is to achieve a state where a white person can believe that they are good, while also believing that discriminatory policies against non-white people are either acceptable or nonexistent. This moral absolution of racism while aggressively building and maintaining racist systems is a duality that exists at the heart of Anglo-American history. From the seventeenth century, Great Britain invaded, starved, and plundered millions of Africans and Asians while maintaining that barbarity was a necessary, civilizing mission. Similarly, the United States built its nation on the backs of black slaves, then, in the nineteenth century, ratified a constitution which declared that all men were equal before God.

This demand for status softened by self-delusion applies across the board of dominant identities. Trump's misogyny is welcomed, or at least not abhorred, by his male supporters. His targeting of transgender soldiers in the US military is welcomed, or at least not abhorred, by his cis supporters. His banning of gay partners of diplomats unless they are married, with the full knowledge that many of them will hail from countries where they cannot be married, is welcomed, or at least not abhorred, by his straight supporters. Trump's pact with his base is a promise of coronation based on identity. A pledge that he will restore the old ways, the old hierarchy of race, gender, nationality, and sexuality. White elites are susceptible to wink logic because it gives them an easy way out, a disclaimer.

Wink logic broadly has two schools. The first innocently invokes patriotism, love for one's country, and the virtues of tradition. The language here paints a picture of an ideal moment in a country's history. In the United States, it would be a suburban scene from the 1950s, an advertorial from before the civil rights movement encroached on the public peace, when blacks were commendably free and yet conveniently separate. It evokes a time of postwar reconstruction, growing affluence, and consumerist plenty. The image is of a white man in a suit and a hat, carrying a briefcase, with a trench coat casually hanging over one arm. He is walking toward his Chevrolet, presumably to go to work, but is making a half-turn toward his suburban split-level to wave goodbye to his wife and child.

The second school appeals not to a glorified, national zenith past, but to a disgraced present. This is where the economy comes in very handy, it is shorthand for something else—the diminishment of the native in their own home, neglected by a metropolitan elite that is preoccupied with women and minorities. Again, Steve Bannon gives us a clear exposition of this strategy: "The Democrats—the longer they talk about identity politics, I got 'em. I want them to talk about racism every day. If the left is focused on race and identity, and we go with economic nationalism, we can crush the Democrats."

Grievance Flipping

The flip side of this coddling of white entitlement is a denigration of other groups' expressions of (real) political grievances and the habit of accusing *them* of racism. In 2016, the *Guardian* writer Sir Simon Jenkins declared that "pale, stale males" such as him were the only remaining group that it is "OK to vilify." When interviewed about the column, he said that the way he feels now, white, male, and above a certain age is sometimes "like what it must have been like to be a black person twenty or thirty years ago." There were no black women (or men, for that matter) with two columns in mainstream newspapers, the *Guardian* and the *Evening Standard*, twenty or thirty years ago. In fact, at the time that Sir Simon made his comments, there was not a single black woman columnist writing full-time for any mainstream British newspaper. He added that black women "slide" into important jobs these days, that he generally feels like he and his cohort are being "squeezed" out of the commentariat, and that there are things that he used to be invited to that he is no longer invited to. At the time of writing, Jenkins remains a columnist at the *Guardian*, his tenure still unthreatened by a "sliding" in of black women.

He ended his column by contradicting all that went before it. "The stales, like the pale males, will have their revenge. They have the spending power, the pensions, the houses; above all, they vote. Call us hideous and disgusting if you want . . . and we shall honor your right to offend us. But prick us and we still bleed. We have our pride. We are going to be around for longer and longer—and we are going to cost you dear."

This switching between pathos and menace, between plaintiveness and threat, between claiming dispossession and then bringing revenge to bear on those you allege are oppressing you with all the might of your vastly superior resources, is the doublethink that lies at the heart of the identity politics myth.

The writer Lionel Shriver manages an even more impressive contortion of logic by accusing non-whites both of racism and of triggering it in others. In a 2018 article in the British magazine the *Spectator*, she argued that a newfound attachment to race by white people was the responsibility of other racial minorities who "have whipped up racial antagonism, encouraged nakedly anti-white bombast and ushered in a glaring double standard that's unsustainable. You cannot have black identity politics, and Latino identity politics, without conjuring the pastel version." This is a myth. The reversal of that sentence, with the pastel version conjuring up the others, is the reality. "The sleeping giant of white identity politics?" she asks. "Thanks to misguided hard-left activism, it's woke."

But Shriver and her compatriots are the ones who have been sleeping. Blaming identity politics for triggering white people has been, as mythical tales usually are, deployed for a long time. Like political correctness, the moment women, racial, and sexual minorities began to ask for equality, the establishment heralded these demands as a successful revolution before the movement had made any inroads. Surveying the media and publishing landscape after the 2016 election, one would not be blamed for thinking that Hillary Clinton and Barack Obama had invented identity politics, as opposed to it being a foundational feature of American politics.

Ashley Jardina, assistant professor of political science at Duke University and author of the book *White Identity Politics*, agrees that people who think of defensive identity politics as corrosive have no understanding of America's history. "Social scientists have been studying it since at least the 1950s," she told me. "Since public opinion polling isolated the union vote, the Catholic vote. It just so happens that race is a major cleavage in the US. But identity politics, as far as the civil rights and women's movements, was politically effective. Black political activity is equal to or surpasses white." Identity politics, she stresses, is not an "incidental and unfortunate outcome" of politics. It is central to it. White entitlement dictated the pejorative view of civil rights movements. When white people refused to share, "bad" identity politics, as practiced by others, was born. Defensive identity politics has always been the way discrete groups of people advanced—successfully—their interests in a society where aggressive identity politics by the majority has resisted their integration.

White Democrat elites have been forced to pay attention to the dangerous effects of white entitlement because for the first time in a long time, passive white identity politics has not worked in their favor. This time, white identity politics ushered in a Republican president with whom they share no establishment interests, intellectual synergy, or networks. A white vote for Trump alarms Democrats more than a white vote for George W. Bush because the former's white supremacy is explicit, ungentrified, expressed by someone not cut from the same cloth as the rest of the political establishment that includes both Republicans and Democrats. Trump's white voters implicate all white Americans across classes. But white elites could not countenance that their own were part of this nationalist movement; it had to be the other whites, the poor ones, those going through some terrible crisis, and so the economic deprivation reasoning again won. Adam Serwer of the *Atlantic* calls this the "Calamity Thesis," the belief that "Trump's election was the direct result of some great, unacknowledged social catastrophe—the opioid crisis, free trade, a decline in white Americans' life expectancy—heretofore ignored by cloistered elites in their coastal bubbles." The irony, he points out, is that "the Calamity Thesis is by far the preferred white-elite explanation for Trumpism and is frequently invoked in arguments among elites as a way of accusing other elites of being out of touch."

The only thing white elites are out of touch with is the pervasiveness of white identity politics. There are many expressions of this white political activity. At its most basic, it is a yearning for, and a covetousness of, status based on race. At its most sophisticated, it is the means by which a complicated infrastructure ensures the spoils of whiteness are maintained.

White identity politics is nothing as crude as conscious racism, of course, although, by definition, to pursue political goals that will come at the expense of other races is a sort of passive racism, just not the zealous, knowing kind. It is more a preservation of currency. The black studies scholar George Lipsitz calls this "the possessive investment in whiteness." Whiteness, he argues, has a "cash value" because it "accounts for advantages that come to individuals through profits made from housing secured in discriminatory markets through the unequal educational opportunities available to children of different races, through insider networks that channel employment opportunities to the relatives and friends of those who have profited most from present and past racial discrimination, and especially through inter-generational transfers of inherited wealth that pass on the spoils of discrimination to succeeding generations." He adds: "White Americans are encouraged to invest in whiteness to remain true to an identity that provides them with resources, power and opportunity." A white identity is a trust fund, and its currency is grievance that is stolen from others.

The Tool—Universalism

If there was a pithy way to summarize the harmful identity politics myth, it would be with the anti–Black Lives Matter slogan, "All Lives Matter." Like the heavily memed "economic anxiety" trope, "All Lives Matter" has become facetious shorthand, an eye roll, calling out logic that swerves the issue by using "whataboutery." "All Lives Matter" invokes universalism, the belief that we should care and advocate for universal rights that affect everyone, such as job security and access to healthcare, rather than tribal ones. Universalists believe that fixating on specific groups' grievances fractures community relations and, in general, compromises the ability to politically mobilize the voting public in the direction of one political party.

I began this chapter with the death of George Floyd and the body count of violent policing and white supremacy because what happened after his death, an uprising of African Americans and indeed, black people all over the world, was immediately discredited by pointing to the damage caused by the protests, and the fact that the protests ignored white people who are also killed by the police. Every time there's a death of a black person at the hands of the police, a chorus of voices lines up to proclaim that this death is not race related, because police in America also kill whites with the same level of random violence that they do black people. The issue, these voices say, is violence, full stop. America is just a violent place. Black people should stop taking violence so personally. Numbers on police killings are parsed and statistics offered, even though absolute numbers are not the relevant metric, but the rate of killings. According to the *New York Times*, Minneapolis police used force against black people at seven times the rate they used it against whites.

Community violence correlations are presented. Some of the efforts to minimize race as a factor extend all the way to claiming, as did Zaid Jilani in *Quillette*, that, yes, it is to be conceded that there is an elevated death rate of African Americans at the hands of the police, but that it is actually not related to race at all, but to the fact that violent crime is more rife within African American communities. Even if that was the case, the fact that there is more violent crime in African American communities is in itself a societal, economic, and culturally produced phenomenon, and if anything, supports the points of the Black Lives Matter movement. The academic John McWhorter called the view that African Americans die for crimes that whites do not an oversimplified "meme." But the BLM "meme" never excluded white deaths, never claimed that whites do not die, never denied that they do. It simply pointed out—and this is a reasonable observation considering the overwhelming evidence— that the threat is higher for black people. The protests, the campaigns, the slogans, they are situated in a history and context where a minority with much less political and economic capital is profiled, harassed, and killed. But by the time we are in the weeds of this discussion, as we are now, the point has been lost. Where was I again? Oh yes. Black Lives Matter.

Then there is the criticism of the means of protest. Every time the questions are the same. What does protesting achieve other than make others feel threatened—what about those others? What does rioting achieve, other than encourage the looting and damaging of property and businesses of people who had no hand in any killing? What about those "small business owners"—another classic euphemism? And consider the optics, how do you expect to build common cause with others, how do you expect to build alliances with white people who will now associate race activism with violence? What about them? Be smart, consider the long game, there is a system in this country, use your vote and exercise democracy rather than let emotion get the better of you.

Soon, not even these arguments are made, as riot mischief is then seized upon as a reason to dismiss the legitimacy of the cause altogether, and the central point becomes about security, anarchy, control, the safety of our streets. Send in the troops. As happened after the George Floyd attacks, in a matter of days, the center of gravity was successfully shifted from the grievances *of* black people, to the safety of the nation *from* black people who are demanding special dispensation to pillage and loot. The late George Floyd's name became an incantation, invoked by Trump to shame black protestors—"THUGS"—for "dishonoring his memory." His death was stolen from African Americans and gifted to the rest of the nation in general, and whites in particular. His death, his noble sacrifice, like that of Martin Luther King Jr. before, was removed from its service to black anger and victimhood. Floyd's tragedy was appropriated by the "all lives matter" principle, the lives that have the right to live without the fear of protests and riots. And so, the message of black lives mattering becomes smeared, ghettoized, and obscured.

This is what universalism achieves, the undermining of legitimate campaigns for equity. It sidesteps specific concerns by dismissing them as special treatment tantrums, thus invalidating them or avoiding engaging with them. "All Lives Matter" does not only suggest that black lives are not lost more brutally and more frequently than white lives, it suggests that to care about black lives is to do so at the expense and exclusion of others. And like all tools, it is not new. In 1991, the American historian C. Vann Woodward wrote: "The cult of ethnicity and its zealots have put at stake the American tradition of a shared commitment to common ideals and its reputation for assimilation, for making a 'nation' of nations."

If there is a criticism to be made of how Democrats pursued identity politics, it is that the party has done so in acts of tokenism since the big electoral conversions of the 1960s. The loyalty of blacks and other people of color to the left is taken for granted and gestured toward without there being any substantive engagement. Hillary Clinton's buzzwords "intersectionality" and "privilege" may have turned off some voters, but they failed to win over others. This kind of political rhetoric, which is heavy on what people perceive as woke language but light on action, puts everyone off. Minorities feel patronized, majorities feel that politics is becoming balkanized and fractured. And so, calls for universal language, universal agendas, and universal "All Lives Matter" campaigns grow louder. These calls to ditch the appeals to identity are strong because identity is so sub-

jective and identity grievances so varied. You cannot achieve mass
political traction by appealing to single identity concerns—unless
that identity is in the majority, as is the case with white identity politics in America. You can see this frustration with the intangibility of
identity in the works of thinkers who have weighed in to the debate
since 2016. In his 2018 book *Identity: Contemporary Identity Politics
and the Struggle for Recognition*, Francis Fukuyama pines for a time
when the nation-state was the unit of identity. In the same year, phi-
losopher Kwame Anthony Appiah asserted in his book *The Lies That
Bind* that identity is "imagined." Unable to conceive of coalitions of
inequality as the way forward, people reach for universal values that
are not relevant when people are disenfranchised. How can someone develop any national patriotism and pride if they feel that their
country does not respect them?

Going back twenty years to 1998, critical theorist Nancy Fra-
ser pointed out that identity politics is used as a derogatory term
because the implication is that gender, race, and sexuality are seen
as ephemeral, flimsy, imagined, or cultural. Class relations, on the
other hand, as political theorist Jonathan Dean explained, "in the
eyes of the identity politics critic, exhibit a depth, profundity and
materiality that 'mere identity' lacks. Furthermore, the alleged universalism of class is contrasted with the narrow, sectional concerns
characteristic of so-called identity politics." This is how the left falls
down again and enables the right—as with the political correctness
and free speech crisis myths—by remaining narrowly obsessed with
the abstract principles of a fight rather than what is actually happening on the ground.

Class fundamentally is about inequality; identity politics is about aspiring to universalism by way of vanquishing inequalities. Economic inequality and identity are inseparable. What is missed by those who are blind to this intersection is that historically, activism based on identity marginalization has been the most successful way by which class concerns were addressed and lasting economic mobility was secured. For example, only by campaigning for the admission of black students into universities could they be promoted into white-collar jobs. The universalism argument assumes that minorities are no longer discriminated against in clear and discrete ways that can be addressed by targeted activism. And so now we must put down tools and hold hands for the only remaining cause that should bind us, whatever that is. For some it is nationalism, for others it is class. Universalism is a cousin of the "progress" myth where women have achieved all the technical legislation wins that can be achieved. Universalism logic imagines successes that are nonexistent.

Defensive identity politics is not at odds with universalism, it just changes the order, putting the horse before the cart: it is a step toward universalism, a building of coalitions. Without identity politics that addresses structural change, rather than advocates for token seats at the table or on the bookshelf, there is no common cause. All lives do matter, but the dangers they face are specific—and where those dangers fall along the lines of identity, it makes no sense to treat them in any other way apart from activism through that identity. As the members of the Combahee River Collective found out all those years ago, no one else is going to do it for you, so push your own cause and find *allies*.

When you are attacked as a Jew, you respond as a Jew.

George Floyd's murder demonstrates that, of all the myths, the identity politics one shows the clearest path to danger. We simply miss the menace of aggressive white identity politics if we refuse to pathologize it, dismissing its most violent manifestations as anomalies, and its political mobilizations as benignly economic. There is a threat to cohesion and there is a fracturing of universal causes, but it's not coming from where the myth is saying it is. In 2018, the *New York Times* reported that US law enforcement has failed to see the threat of white nationalism and is struggling to stop it as it had caught them unawares. That failure to take the white nationalist threat seriously spanned the two full decades since 9/11. "In the atmosphere of willful indifference," the report stated, "a virulent movement has grown and metastasized."

It could be argued that the *New York Times* itself "missed it," so busy was it with reinforcing white entitlement narratives.

Yes, ideally, we should strive to appeal to all and create a solidarity based on common goals. But this ideal world where an identity hierarchy does not exist is a fiction that only exists in the minds of those more preoccupied with the control aspect of universalism— which is about being able to direct people en masse and mobilize them politically. The myth that identity is something that only others do, not white people, is one that has enabled politicians to play on white racial grievance across classes while their liberal counterparts made the right noises in the direction of minorities but never genuinely engaged with their causes.

In a 2018 article for the website the *Outline*, US writer Sean McElwee summarized why, if liberals do not in fact embrace identity politics, they have no future: "There is simply no electoral benefit to be gained from abandoning identity politics because voters are increasingly sorted in such a way that those who support economically progressive policies are also supportive of racial justice and gender equity." He concluded, "The path forward will require an understanding of how deeply liberation from patriarchy, white supremacy, and capitalism are intertwined."

Defensive identity politics is not the problem, it is, in fact, the only way forward.

5

The Myth of National Exceptionalism

What we choose to forget often reveals the limits of justice in our collective imaginations. What we choose to memorialize reflects what we actually value.

—*Eddie S. Glaude Jr.*

If you take down monuments to evildoers, people will forget the dark parts of history, which is why nobody knows who Hitler was.

—*Philomena Cunk*

There is no mainstream account of a country's history that is not a collective delusion. The present cannot be celebrated without the past being edited. For the United States to believe in its American dream, in its land of opportunity, where all men are equal before God and able to achieve whatever they wish through toil and virtue, it cannot be acknowledged that it was built on the genocide of Native Americans and the enslavement of Africans and Europe's poor. If the United Kingdom is to have a sense of pride in its contemporary self, there is no way it can be acknowledged that the country was built on global expansion, resource extraction, and slavery. For Sudan, my country of birth, to believe that it is a unique blend of African and Arab tribes that have thrived by the River Nile for millennia, it cannot be acknowledged that it has been engaged in ethnic warfare for the better part of a century.

Every country has its airbrush. Some airbrushes are universal banal fictions; others are central to a hubris that is internally corrosive and externally predatory, feeding domestic division and global aggression.

And so, our historical heroes too must be edited. Everything from their human rights records and prejudices, to their minor foibles and imperfections, is cleansed. An assassinated Egyptian president is remembered as a pious Muslim, even though he had poured himself a stiff glass of Scotch whisky after every evening prayer. Barack Obama is the healthy basketball-playing president but was reportedly a chain smoker. His image is that of swaggering virtue, giving a fist bump to janitors and channeling the conscience of the nation when he shed tears for the young victims of gun crime, all while he rained hell on civilians in an intensified drone campaign in Pakistan, Somalia, and Yemen. In Sudan, Al Mahdi, the glorified founder of the first Sudanese quasi-nation state and vanquisher of the Anglo-Egyptian occupation, led an army which, as well as defeating the occupying forces, plundered, murdered, raped, and sold into slavery tens of thousands of its own people. This was a man who believed that he was the messiah, sent by Allah himself to purify his land. He is revered in history books and his progeny continue to hold political sway. If he were born in present-day Sudan and announced he was God's messenger, he would be tried for apostasy.

The past is rewritten in broad strokes, but the present is revised in small amendments or omissions. George W. Bush, a president who, in his time, was seen as a reckless warmonger and the intellectually challenged beneficiary of a trust fund, became the subject of a curious rebrand that began precisely at Donald Trump's inauguration. Something about seeing Bush looking like a mischievous schoolboy unselfconsciously perplexed by Trump's speech—after which he reportedly said to Hillary Clinton that it was "some crazy shit"—immediately recast him. Bush, compared to Trump, was a competent member of the political establishment. He launched one of the most disastrous wars in the Middle East with no plan or reliable intelligence—but at least he wasn't this rambling, sloppy bigot.

Anglo-American history is particularly prone to such fictions, so strong is its dependence on a foundational myth for its sense of identity. In *White Trash: The 400-Year Untold History of Class in America*, Nancy Isenberg repeatedly skewers America's imaginary history. It was not, contrary to conventional wisdom, founded by the pious pilgrims of England, but by successive waves of Europe's destitute sent to exile and indentured servitude. These settlers did not thrive. "Americans' sketchy understanding of the nation's colonial beginnings reflects the larger cultural impulse to forget—or at least gloss over—centuries of dodgy decisions, dubious measures, and outright failures," she writes. "Most settlers in the seventeenth century did not envision their forced exile as the start of a 'Citty upon a Hill.'"

Paintings of the "Founding Fathers" were changed as the lens of history shifted; they became more English and grander as time went by. This is the myth of history, that of the virtuous origin. Not successive facts and moments frozen in time, but a painting touched and retouched to reflect back to society its sense of stature and purpose. A sort of Dorian Gray reversed, where the painting remains impeccable as the real-life version grows gnarled and grotesque.

The whitewashing of the history of colonialism and slavery is integral to the belief that there is something inherently noble about ex-colonial Europe and the US. The myth of a virtuous origin is the strongest, most corrosive myth of all. Nations fail to reflect on themselves when they believe there is something special about them. Countries repeat disastrous mistakes when they are convinced that their essence is fundamentally sound. There is a straight line that runs from this belief and another: that there is an essential moral superiority about a white race that has managed to create material wealth by virtue of its own enterprise, rather than the leveraging of poor and black labor both in their home countries and imported against their will.

The myth feeds the assumption that there is a continuum of enlightenment, briefly interrupted by two world wars, two aberrations, that lasts to this day. The truth is that Anglo-American history—and to a similar extent, Western European history—is founded on both the elevation of whiteness to cult status in order to instill a sense of superior national identity and the pursuit of conflict abroad to confer a sense of purpose at home.

The Prussian military theorist Carl von Clausewitz coined the aphorism that war is the continuation of politics by other means. From the late 1800s, imperialist expansion into the Americas, Africa, and the Indian subcontinent was the continuation of domestic politics by foreign means. Take Cecil Rhodes, a man whose life is a testament to the happy marriage of expansionist white supremacy and capitalist success. In 1870, his jaunt as a teenager to South Africa for health reasons resulted in him founding both De Beers and the South African territory of Rhodesia. He offered a clear, unapologetic summary of outsourcing. In his view, imperialism was a "solution for the social problem." He said, "In order to save the forty million inhabitants of the United Kingdom from a bloody civil war, we colonial statesmen must acquire new lands to settle the surplus population, to provide new markets for the goods produced in the factories and mines." He believed that "if you want to avoid civil war, you must become imperialists."

The myth of national exceptionalism is nourished by what is essentially state propaganda via academic curricular *blind spots, popular culture fetishization*, themes of *restoration,* calls for *contextualization* (it was all a different time, you see), and a *balance sheet* analysis.

A Nation's Blind Spot

The way many countries curate their taught histories is an exercise in mass consensual dishonesty. If a country retelling its story were a person recollecting a heavily edited and falsified view of the past, they would broadly—and accurately—be considered an unreliable witness to their own experience. There is no mention of Al Mahdi's massacres in the Sudanese school history curricula. In Saudi Arabia, one of the most significant and bloody events in its history, the storming of the Great Mosque of Mecca in 1979 by another Mahdi-type figure, is not only absent from the public records but any book that makes any mention of it is banned. Juhayman al-Otaybi was a Saudi soldier and militant who led an invasion of Islam's holiest site, believing that it was his religious duty to rid the Kingdom of its monarchy for failing in its holy duty to rule Saudi Arabia according to the correct principles of Islam. His attempt failed after a bloody clash with authorities, and he was arrested and executed. The siege of Mecca determined the shape of politics in the country in the decades that followed, and to stave off further threats of political religious insurrection and save its neck, the royal family forged a pact with the religious establishment and its powerful mullahs. I spent most of my life in the Arab world until the age of twenty-five, some of those years in Saudi Arabia, but only learned of the siege of Mecca when I moved to Europe. When my mother came to visit me in the UK for the first time, I gave her a book recounting the incident and its fallout. A college professor who thought she knew a thing or two about history, she was left stunned by the extent of the suppression. My little sister, a medical doctor who grew up in Saudi Arabia and received her entire education in the Saudi state schooling system, still does not believe the siege of Mecca ever happened.

Not many are shocked to learn this, or that, for example, Chinese history books omit the Cultural Revolution's purges. But the assumption is not extended to American history, which, in reality, is just as calculating and subjective.

Until 2015, certain textbooks in some US state school syllabuses told students that those who were brought over from Africa were "workers," rather than groups of chained slaves that included children. One textbook, created by academic publishing giant McGraw-Hill for the state of Texas, under a section called "Patterns of Immigration," stated that the Atlantic slave trade brought "millions of workers from Africa to the southern United States to work on agricultural plantations." A fifteen-year-old student took a picture of the text and sent it to his mother, who then complained, prompting the withdrawal of the text. The publisher said it was an "error." This "error" had been missed by not just teachers, but also textbook reviewers at the Texas Board of Education—who would have demanded and commissioned such content—and all the editors at McGraw-Hill. Not only did the caption erase the violence and coercion of slavery, it collapsed the entire history of slavery, the reason for the presence of an entire demographic in the United States, into a "pattern of migration."

There is a long, sinister history to these sorts of "errors," and a more innocent but no less damaging recent history. American accounts of slavery, the civil war, and abolition were deliberately crafted to launder the reputation of the country to new generations. In the early twentieth century, unflattering depictions of the South were excised or prevented from being entered in the history books by such figures as Mildred Lewis Rutherford. A historian and teacher, she wrote a guidebook called *A Measuring Rod to Test Text Books, and Reference Books in Schools, Colleges and Libraries*, which was published in 1920. In it, she detailed the rules on what should be allowed in history books. "Reject a book that says the South fought to hold her slaves," she wrote. "Reject a book that speaks of the slaveholder of the South as cruel and unjust to his slaves."

Sometimes, history is written not by the victors, but by the losers. In a sense, Confederates such as Rutherford, still smarting from their defeat in the Civil War, merely continued the war by other means, carefully crafting a story about benevolent slave owners and thriving slaves. Others went further, arguing that the abolition of slavery did nothing but create social tension that would be eased only via the establishing of another system that formalized racial hierarchy. The effort was not limited to individuals. Challenging the Reconstruction era in which slavery was abolished and Confederate secession ended became a whole school of thought. The Dunning School, named after Columbia professor William A. Dunning, was a group of scholars who argued that equality between the races was unnatural, and that the abolition of slavery had ushered in an era of impossible coexistence between whites and blacks. In 1987, Dunning wrote that "the abolitionist fever was the root of the trouble in the South." Slavery "had been a modus vivendi," an efficient arrangement that was required for races to live alongside each other in as little tension as possible. With the removal of this structure, a chaos was unleashed, necessitating a new system that "must in essence express the same fact of racial inequality."

The hangover of these efforts to resist emancipation and racial equality is strong. Academic curricula did not improve radically after the 1920s. In a 2019 survey of high school history books throughout the twentieth century, the *Washington Post* found that right until the 1970s not only did school curricula across the country not teach students about the history of slavery, they often invented a fictional account. In one Alabama textbook, students were told that "with all the drawbacks of slavery, it should be noted that slavery was the earliest form of social security in the United States." In another, in Virginia, students learned that the state provided "a better life for the Negroes than did Africa. In his new home, the Negro was far away from the spears and war clubs of enemy tribes. He had some of the comforts of civilized life."

Today, such bold apologizing has been removed, but it has been replaced with silence and neutral descriptions of "workers" from

Africa contributing to the "migration patterns" of the United States. Less out of conspiracy to suppress a narrative, but in some cases out of awkwardness and fear, because even though slavery may be in the past, its legacy is firmly in the present. When it comes to coming to grips with the grievous sin of slavery and its long tail of cruelty, segregation, and current-day discrimination, "the past is never dead," as William Faulkner wrote, "it's not even past."

A 2018 study by the SPLC's Teaching Tolerance project discovered that Civil War literacy among US high school students was poor, with only 8 percent citing slavery as the central cause of the war. Overall, only 44 percent were aware of the fact that slavery was legal in all colonies during the American Revolution. Less than half knew that slavery was ended formally only after a constitutional amendment. The stress on individual liberty as the motor of American exceptionalism only works if society is free and flat. The whole idea of America does not work if slavery, both synthetic in the form of indebted Europeans and actual free labor from Africa, becomes too central to the story. Much like Donald Trump, America is not a self-made man, it is a country that benefited from a trust fund gifted to it by cheap labor and exploitation, a trust fund that created such low-margin wealth that its dividends are still being distributed today.

In surveying how young black Americans felt about their education, I spoke to two African American brothers who had studied in California. In their midtwenties, they only recently became attuned to the gaping hole in their knowledge about slavery, its evils, and how long it lasted. "It was just a rarely touched-upon subject," one of them, Mohamed Marghani, told me. "You just learn about the Civil War battles. You just learn that slavery happened, it was bad, and then Lincoln fixes it." He laughs. Then he goes on to say: "It's actually insane, and why we're so bad with race."

Part of the problem is that there is no unified national requirement for teaching social studies and United States history, only for mathematics and reading. African American teachers shared with me their frustration at how helpless they feel. One teacher in Washington, DC, said, "There's only so much we can do without going completely off curriculum, and then it looks like you have some political agenda."

This has left the country not only ignorant of its past but unable to grapple with its present, unable to understand why or how it came to be, or even to agree on the basic established facts of its events. Is it any wonder then, that race protests still rock America every few years? And that the response often questions the validity of the grievance?

Memorializing racism

There are more than 1,500 public monuments and memorials to the Confederacy in the United States, over half of which are monuments and statues. Almost half of those monuments and statues are in Georgia, Virginia, and North Carolina. The pretense that the latter are not glorifications of the actions of racist figures in the past, merely records of the state's "heritage," was shattered once and for all by the Charlottesville rally of 2017. A march against the removal of the statue of Robert E. Lee—incidentally, commissioned in the early twentieth-century period of palliating confederate loss—became a unifying event for the forces of the right. It was a who's who of American racism, bringing together neo-Nazis, white supremacists, anti-Semites, and Islamophobes. When the march turned violent and a counterprotestor was killed by a white supremacist, it became clear that lurking alongside arguments that those statues shouldn't be removed because that would constitute erasing America's racist history were others that didn't want them to be removed because they wanted to glorify that racist history.

Even those who don't believe that they are paying homage to racism by keeping such busts and statues still come at the issue from the perspective of someone for whom slavery and the Civil War have no emotional or psychological impact. They can afford to see history as simply an account that should not be disturbed or edited. They can afford to see the statues and monuments of slavery as records, and not homages. To be a black person under the gaze of such memorials is to feel keenly the fact that their own polity venerates their oppression.

Rabah Taha, an African American resident of Washington, DC, who graduated from the University of Virginia, told me how when the Charlottesville rally took place, she was not surprised. In fact, she felt it was a long time coming: "The white and black student populations at college were worlds apart, as apart as they could have been without formal segregation." As a black student, she felt she occupied a parallel world to that of the white students, that their perceptions of history and the country they live in were irreconcilable. Classes they shared which touched on memorials or history quickly became awkward and tense, with white students who had no common cause with those who marched in Charlottesville seeing the memorializing of generals and soldiers who had fought to keep black people enslaved as merely a part of history that shouldn't be judged in hindsight. It caused, for her, a profound alienation from her country.

The absenting of an honest, nationwide, studied account of slavery has allowed these cleavages to grow unchecked, reverberating subtly and dangerously throughout the years. There was never a reckoning. Germany invented a uniquely German compound noun to describe the process of that reckoning—*Vergangenheitsbewälti-gung*—of learning from and coming to terms with the past so that its crimes are never repeated. America never went through this process. It never purged itself. The institution of slavery was central in the crafting of the Constitution. Its abolition necessitated a constitutional amendment. It has carved the shape of American capitalism, defining the contours of class and labor today. And yet where it should sit at the heart of the American story remains a vacuum filled, almost entirely, by a self-aggrandizing American popular culture that continues to absolve the nation of its crimes.

Popular Culture Fetishization

Growing up outside of the United States in the '80s but still reared on a diet of American popular culture, I got the impression that broadly, only two significant historical events had ever happened to Americans: slavery, and the Vietnam War. Two books could be found in pretty much all the homes across the new postcolonial, educated class in sub-Saharan Africa—*Roots* and *The Autobiography of Malcom X*. They were, to me, the only works where black narratives and protagonists were entered into the record. Everything else, from *Gone with the Wind* to *Little House on the Prairie*, depicted slavery and the enslaved as bucolic background figures. All that endured, all that imprinted on a young black girl's mind while viewing *Gone with the Wind* was Scarlett O'Hara's dresses. In other movies where slavery or discrimination was the central theme, there always seemed to be a white protagonist treading some moral arc; the lawyer in *Amistad* who comes around to seeing slaves as humans and not as commercial property, the father in *To Kill a Mockingbird*, the journalist in *Cry Freedom*.

It seemed that what was really being memorialized was not the pain visited upon slaves, nor the efforts they themselves made to secure their liberation, but the entire institution of slavery as a vehicle for America's moral awakening. A benevolent white man was a deus ex machina who plucked the slave out of their plight at the eleventh hour—Brad Pitt's role in *12 Years a Slave* is a classic of this genre. Films that depict post-slavery suffering of black characters feature the same flattening of the black story to serve as backdrop to some sort of white heroism. In some cases, the white heroism is shoehorned in even in adaptations of real stories where none existed. In *Hidden Figures*, a dramatization of a real-life story about three African American women working at NASA in 1961, Kevin Costner, who plays the boss of one of the women, stands up for her right to use the whites-only bathroom, and allows her into Mission Control to view the launch of the project she worked on. Neither scene ever took place.

Just as slavery and the discrimination that followed it were turned into a white story, so was the other formative experience in America's modern psyche, the Vietnam War, turned into a tale of American forbearance rather than loss. An entire genre of film in the 1970s and '80s features the figure of the lone returning Vietnam vet, bearing his physical and psychological scars. Brutalized in Vietnam, he is shunned by the community he returns to, then spat on as he is let down by his own people and the government which has tossed him aside. But somehow, he prevails. Hollywood reproduced the myth of an inherently good individual American who not only battled others, but his own government. And so, even though the Vietnam War was a bloody nose for the idea of a good and strong America, the valiant American soldier became the enduring image of the war; John Rambo in *Rambo*, Anthony Curtis in *Dead Presidents*, and of course, Travis Bickle in *Taxi Driver*.

The morality of war, slavery, and atrocities committed in Vietnam is rarely addressed. The war on terror received the same treatment, its story told via individual American heroes. The vehicles of this anthology are lone, intrepid Americans, carriers of the "good American DNA." Carrie Mathison in *Homeland*, Tony Mendez in *Argo*, and Agent Maya in *Zero Dark Thirty* embody the spirit of America. Out in unfamiliar territory, working against the dark mischief of the foreigner and the political machinations, manipulations, and cynicism of Washington, they carry a kernel of goodness that proves that the software of America is sound. Theirs is the certainty that runs through America's appraisal of its own cultural history. The American audience comes away with its sense of superiority intact. But it's not a vulgar supremacy, it is served with a side of classy humility that America is an imperfect place. It is a genius formula that perpetuates American historical exceptionalism. Commercially it has been a box office hit. And Hollywood has patted itself on the back via a host of awards and baubles that prove its liberal credentials.

Some of the displacing of America's moral failings is more cynical. In his book *The Spitting Image: Myth, Memory, and the Legacy of Vietnam*, Jerry Lembcke reveals the established perception that anti-war activists spat at and demeaned Vietnam vets was largely a

fiction. In fact, the opposite was true. Seeing them as victims themselves of an unjust war, anti-war activists and organizations largely
supported Vietnam vets, who in turned had come to share some
of the anti-war protestors' political positions. The famous "spitting
image" was a result of successful efforts by the Nixon administration to paint the anti-war movement as unpatriotic and traitorous.
By doing so, Nixon moved the failure of the war and the burden of
low morale onto war dissenters and away from the government. In
1992, the director of the Connelly Library and curator of the Vietnam War Collection at LaSalle University placed the spitting myth
on a list of the "Top Six Myths" about Vietnam.

In part because of the spitting myth, the focus shifted. The Vietnam vet was pathologized as suffering from PTSD and drug abuse,
a pitiful figure on the fringes of society. These accounts served to
silence and stigmatize public dissent against foreign wars. In the
paper "Who Supports the Troops? Vietnam, the Gulf War, and the
Making of Collective Memory," the authors Thomas D. Beamish,
Harvey Molotch, and Richard Flacks found that blaming the loss
in Vietnam on Americans at home and returning vets chilled and
blunted opposition to the Gulf War. "Gulf War opponents," the paper
stated, "including many Vietnam-era anti-war activists, themselves
accepted, sometimes enthusiastically, the need to express support
for the troops. Gulf War opponents saw supporting the troops as
necessary to overcome resentment based on the sins of Vietnam-era
activists."

These powerful popular culture narratives, particularly in the
absence of sufficient academic account of America's slavery at home
and warmongering abroad, create a soft-focus version of the country.
Of beautiful plantations run by highborn slaveowners, and of heroic

brotherhoods forged in the field of battle. This bankable nostalgia is not a fad, it is a culmination. And it is not just a part of popular culture sewn together along with all the pieces of a nation's quilt; it is a singularly defining piece. More melancholia than nostalgia, it adds a state of loss to that of longing. The jeopardy is when that tips into attempts at restoration, of recapturing a past that not only never existed, but in which many suffered and perished, including white Americans, for only a few to flourish. When such distortions dominate the historical narrative, policy blunders and political adventurism are inevitable. And so, the race fissures are never healed because they are never properly acknowledged, and the foreign quagmires, from Vietnam through to the Gulf War, the Iraq War, and the ongoing war in Afghanistan, continue to claim lives abroad and send body bags home.

America's education gap is a function of a wider state of arrest. Unable to move on, to go through its own *Vergangenheitsbewälti-gung*, the country remains stuck in a loop of recurring racism-related violence, a stubborn and flourishing white supremacist movement, and bloody, pointless foreign interventions in faraway places. Unable to face up to the sins of the past, unable to atone and adjust for them, America's belief in its historical virtue is a near-perfect example of how, when taken too far, myths lead to self-harm.

Restoration—Making America Great Again

Again. In that word is encapsulated all of America's myth of history and its dangers.

When was this previous greatness exactly? It is an imaginary time, a selective montage of past glories. *Again* here means the return to a state of superiority, where America's doctrine of manifest destiny gave the settlers the license to expand westward and annex territory, bringing with them their technology, virtues, and evolved agrarian institutions to civilize the savage. It means to purify and consolidate once more, behind a vision of America that is orderly at home, dominant and destructive abroad, forever expanding, always invoking some high principle for annexation and broadening of influence. This myth has made America less secure. Its foreign meddling has, both pre- and post-9/11, created blowback that is still claiming lives. Its internal contradictions collapse under their own weight. A country that said "give me your poor, your huddled masses" is the same country that, under Trump, separated children from their parents at the border, often forever, and banned legally resident Muslims from entering the country. It is this sense of an inherently good America that gives moral cover to its fundamental, in fact its defining, inequalities. A mythical white and superior America, in which individual liberty thrives and where, as the historian Thomas A. Bailey put it, "the rags to riches dream of a millionaire's blank check [can be found] in every working man's lunch box."

America's externally supremacist attitude cannot be divorced from an internally supremacist one. There is hierarchy. America sits on top globally and a certain type of American sits on top domestically. *Again* is a coded call to purge contemporary society of elements that challenge those who hitherto enjoyed unquestioned status—the changing demographics due to immigration, equal rights for women, and cultural accommodation. All the developments that diminish the spoils of entitlement. *Again*, it is a message to the rest of the world that American military might and interventionism are back.

Externalization is an important component of the appeal *again*. Since World War I and after the Great Depression in the 1930s, America has derived its self-worth—after being dragged out of its isolationism by the 1941 Japanese attack on Pearl Harbor—from engaging in military campaigns and standoffs. The country adopted its own version of Cecil Rhodes's belief that civil war at home is to be avoided by engaging in imperialist ventures abroad. Imperialism is both a commercial boon and a fillip, a valve that can be loosened or tightened to relieve pressure as required.

It is terrifying to be at the other end of the pipe. The Clinton–Lewinsky scandal broke when I was at university in Khartoum in 1998. I remember watching the news coverage on Al Jazeera and flinching when the newsreader said the Arabic word for "sexual relations." My face burned as my father and his brothers pretended they did not hear the reference. A few weeks later, I was in the yard of our house when suddenly the earth began to tremble, and the windows vibrated. I remember thinking it was perhaps the sound and impact of a car tire exploding, a common event in the heat of Sudan, but this one shook the house.

The next morning, we heard that a pharmaceutical factory called Al-Shifa had been bombed by the Americans. It seemed so far-fetched that for hours I did not believe it, thinking that it was just government chicanery or something more banal, like faulty factory wiring. Sudan was not at war—Khartoum was a peaceful, sleepy city that had never seen open combat. The country was on a terrorism blacklist, but it seemed implausible that it was conducting terrorism business in the heart of the city's downtown, and certainly not anything that required bombing. But the Al-Shifa plant had in fact been taken out on the direct orders of President Clinton. The strike was allegedly in retaliation for Osama bin Laden's bombings of the US embassies in Kenya and Tanzania. The Clinton administration, on flimsy evidence, had eliminated one of Sudan's major medical suppliers. It claimed that the plant was "actually a disguised chemical weapons factory" and that "soil samples taken outside the plant had shown the presence of a substance known as EMPTA, whose only function was to make the nerve gas VX."

The plant, it was claimed, "was heavily guarded and it showed a suspicious lack of ordinary commercial activities." Some US officials even claimed that bin Laden had financed it. These claims turned out to be false. During the political fallout of the bombing, I could not get the timing out of my mind. Because the missiles came days after Monica Lewinsky's testimony before a grand jury, it was hard not to see the Al-Shifa attack as a display for the benefit of audiences back home. Perhaps it was designed to distract from Clinton's televised address, or to portray an administration taking decisive action at a time when America was rattled by previous terrorist attacks. Regardless, we—me, standing in the yard as the missiles struck—were a headline to galvanize Americans at home. It's a hard lesson to forget. To feel the earth move beneath your feet and know that your entire life and world are collateral damage, a stage for a man far away, a man who was feeling helpless because of a bombing that your country had nothing to do with, and cornered because he abused his power by having an affair with a young intern, then was caught lying about it.

This random aggression wasn't a one-off. In 1998, a letter was sent to President Clinton from people associated with the neoconservative think tank Project for the New American Century (PNAC)—the breadcrumb trail always leads to the think tank, and then to the money. Formed in early 1997, PNAC's purpose, once the fancy descriptions were stripped away, was to maintain American hegemony in the world. Almost a decade after the fall of the Soviet Union, something was needed, in the absence of communism, to give the US a sense of purpose *again*. The letter read:

> *We are writing you because we are convinced that current American policy toward Iraq is not succeeding, and that we may soon face a threat in the Middle East more serious than any we have known since the end of the Cold War.... We urge you to seize that opportunity, and to enunciate a new strategy that would secure the interests of the US and our friends and allies around the world. That strategy should aim, above all, at the removal of Saddam Hussein's regime from power.*

The 1991 Gulf War had not gone far enough.

Three years later, many of the letter's signatories, in particular Donald Rumsfeld, Paul Wolfowitz, and Dick Cheney, were to join the George W. Bush administration.

They and others felt that the end of the Cold War, in the early 1990s, had been a lost opportunity for the United States to press the advantage as the world's remaining superpower. The idea was that the US should project itself decisively and preemptively—in case China, Germany, or Japan got any fresh ideas—and establish a sort of Orwellian "war is peace" Pax Americana. After 1989, defense expenditure as a proportion of GDP began to fall in the US. By the year 2000, American spending on defense was at its lowest since World War II. PNAC wanted this to change, lobbying for an increase in spending and even for a new outfit called "US Space Forces" to patrol the globe. (Critics mocked Donald Trump's founding of the "United States Space Force," but the notion was a serious one put forward by Republican hawks decades prior to his presidency.)

In a chilling report from 2000, PNAC members wrote that repositioning the US was a "process of transformation" and that it was "likely to be a long one, absent some catastrophic and catalyzing event—like a new Pearl Harbor." They got their wish. America got its catastrophic and catalytic wake-up. Exactly one year after the report was published, the terrorist attacks of 9/11 happened. Not only did this give such hawks a second stab at the orgy of the first Gulf War, in which Saddam was dominated by a one-hundred-hour Desert Storm and the Arabian Gulf was liberated and secured, it also gave them their opening to press the advantage. For many, 9/11 was a rebuke to those who believed that there should be limits on the US in the global arena. For America to be strong and safe, it had to be everywhere.

Writing in *Salon* in 2018, the political writer Tom Engelhardt described the shock, followed by the rush of bloodlust. "Like their confrères in 1991," he wrote, "the top officials of George W. Bush's administration were initially stunned by the event, but soon found themselves swept up in a mood of soaring optimism about the future of both the Republican Party and American power. Their dream, as they launched what they called the Global War on Terrorism, would be nothing short of creating an eternal *Pax Republicana* in the United States and a similar, never-ending *Pax Americana* first in the Greater Middle East and then on a potentially planetary scale."

In the way Britain has been warped by empire, so has America been warped by the Cold War. The cultural project that was required to craft America's moral exceptionalism made a rewriting of its violent history and scrappy origins not only a necessity but a tool of war. And so, America's fundamental myth splits into two.

The first is the story of Anglo-Saxons striving for self-governance and individual liberty once they fled draconian Europe, and then benignly oversaw slaves until their liberation. Everything conveniently and coherently begins in early seventeenth-century New England. But even this elegant account of settlement was not true. Englishmen settled in Virginia at least two decades before that in the late 1500s. Perry Miller, a Pulitzer Prize–winning Harvard historian who cofounded the field of American studies, was instrumental in forcing this narrative of a New England populated by English men and women of a certain faith and political outlook. According to fellow historian Francis T. Butts, Miller's work was "widely held to provide the standard interpretation of the development of New England culture." After his death, however, Miller's canon fell subject to criticism that he was forcing coherence in order to extrapolate something about the foundational uniqueness of the American character. By his own admission, he "wanted a coherence with which [he] could coherently begin."

Historian Michael Zuckerman wrote that in doing so, Miller "made whole colonies disappear with the wave of a wish," and that "he suggested that early New England afforded an embodiment of American cultural processes an ideal laboratory 'chiefly valuable for its *representative* quality . . . a sort of working model for American history.'"

These working models of American history were reproduced for every era, each reifying the innate nobility, piety, and enterprise of the American prototype. And with every era, the reinforcement of that notion came by way of conflict. The latest working model of American history was forged in the furnaces of the war on ter-ror, whereby a conveniently cartoonish villain, hiding in lairs in the mountains and villages of Afghanistan and Pakistan, hated America for its freedom. America patted itself on the back for hunt-ing him down and executing him, while ignoring the millions of Muslims whose lives were lost as America lashed out incoherently, a whole continent away, in Iraq. Muslims and Islam provided an ersatz communism, a group of values and villains out of central casting and against which America's superiority can come into relief, and which will give it the excuse to extend itself further, pen-etrate deeper into the affairs and lands of other nations.

The second part of America's foundational myth is this pretense that bloody expansionism is a defensive move, a reluctant but deter-mined venture necessitated by the elimination of scheming enemies.

This impulse is not a right-wing or conservative one. Bill Maher exchanges chest bumps with other classical liberals in muscular, freedom-loving expression when it comes to Islam, and is the most outspoken non-right-wing opponent of the religion. Among many other statements, including the ones mentioned earlier, he has called Islam the only "religion that acts like the mafia that will fucking kill you if you say the wrong thing," and has said that "the Muslim world has too much in common with ISIS." Media figures, writers, and academics such as Maher, Sam Harris, and Richard Dawkins enthusiastically signed on to this hatred of Islam, but never made the association between Islamophobia as a continuation of Amer-ica's supremacist history and the bloody campaigns waged against Muslim countries. And so the cycle continues, feeding racial ten-sion at home and stoking conflict abroad to uphold a fictional self-perception of racial superiority and global hegemony.

America's account of its history is a fiction that serves only to uphold these irreconcilable contradictions between its perception of itself and its reality—a nation built on domination abroad and structural inequality at home. The call to make America great *again*, by voting in a man who stands for none of its alleged values and embodies all of its hypocrisies, is the inevitable culmination of that fiction. Americans continue to pay a heavy price for these false beliefs, caught in a permanent state of domestic discord and unnecessary wars. All the while romanticizing an era in the past that was simpler, because the natives, either imported or invaded, were less restive.

This is the danger of reaching to the past to cast a flattering light on the present—the nostalgia informs action and ideology. The past is a simple place; it provides simple solutions to complex, intractable problems. In a sense, there is no *again*, whatever the country or people. There was never a moment in time where a specific culture thrived because it had struck on some golden formula for prosperity and equality. Whether it was the Islamic empire, the Ming dynasty, or the Roman empire, none flourished without slavery, disenfranchisement, oppression of women, and authoritarianism. Most civilizations are, in relative terms, more advanced than the last in technology and law, but not more advanced in absolute terms. What all civilizations share is a denial of the fact that empire-like dominance is achieved at high costs to the less fortunate. America's economic strength today is another version of accomplishment secured at the expense of the poorly paid, the uninsured, and those whose labor rights have been slowly but relentlessly chipped away. There is no *again* for America, or any other nation.

Doublethink is a strong feature of what is required to sustain a myth. One of its main features is the ability to maintain a grievance of humiliation that does not, however, dent a belief in self. The way to sustain this contradictory state of defeat and superiority is to avoid confronting the heart of the failure. And so, it is easier for a white American to blame immigrants for their impoverishment than his own government's economic policies. It is a choice between "I am poor because I am unfortunate"—a wretched state—"I am poor because of a rigged capitalist world order"—a trapped state—and "I am poor because of others less deserving, external governments, and politicians who are too weak to stand up for me"—a victim state. In the last case, something can be done. You can't change the fact of capitalism, you can't change the class and economic state you are born into. But when you are a victim of the "other," it's not your fault. Your misfortune is not a by-product of immutable political patterns, you have volition to change the politicians who conspire against you, leave global treaties, kick out foreigners, and be great again.

The Tool—The Balance Sheet and Contextualization

In Berlin stands a museum named the Topography of Terror. An outdoor and indoor exhibition, its flow is a simple retracing of the administrative side of Nazism and the work of its branches of enforcement—the SS and the police. Moving chronologically through the exhibition, visitors can follow the rise of the Third Reich through to the end of World War II. It is an experience that is hard to describe if one has not visited. Even though there is an audio tour and a thorough description of all the exhibits, there is an absence of narrator. Everything is relayed in the most neutral, factual way, from the copy of the original Final Solution decree, to the mug shots of German resistance members. In the clinical way the exhibition is presented—without editorializing—history is delivered in all its vivid and banal detail. For a guide or narrator to abhor it would be to consign it to a different time when horrible things happened; to excuse it would be to put too much distance between the present and the past. In doing neither, the purpose of the museum has been achieved—what we learn is that it can happen again.

There are three ways of looking at history—as a source of pride, as a source of shame, or as a series of events that inform the present. When history becomes part of identity, when it becomes about a virtuous origin that gives a people an exceptional character, it is no longer history. You can tell when this is happening because history storytellers come into it, discounting this and inflating that, asking for context and a fair appraisal of the good as well as the bad. This is the balance sheet tool. It sets up a false premise, the purpose of which is to turn history into something else, into an achievement, a thing that says something about the quality of a nation's present character. Once the balance sheet tool is wielded it turns history into an account from two sides, trapping those who would like history simply to be demythologized in a binary where there can only be two accounts—history as virtuous origin or history as shame.

The most egregious example of reasoning supported by the balance sheet tool is the removal of Saddam Hussein. The Iraq War was an unmistakable calamity. The reason for wading into it, Hussein's weapons of mass destruction, was a fabrication. And so, the motivation for the war had to be rewritten. There was no way to claim that the initial premise for the invasion—a preemptive strike in the war on terror—was valid, so the only way to redeem the war was to reach for a balance sheet analysis. As Iraq's unraveling became undeniable and it seemed that, in fact, the US invasion was a shot in the arm for local Islamic terrorist organizations, John Bolton began putting scores on the board to balance out the criticism of the war. In 2013, the former ambassador to the United Nations under George W. Bush set out the motivation clearly. Hostility against the war, he wrote, was threatening "to overwhelm, in the public mind, the clear merits of eliminating Iraq's Ba'athist dictatorship."

"Our broad international coalition," he continued, "accomplished its military mission with low casualties and great speed, sending an unmistakable signal of power and determination throughout the Middle East and around the world. Despite all the criticism of what happened after Saddam's defeat, these facts are indisputable."

Those facts were indisputable indeed, because nobody was disputing them. What was being disputed was whether the anarchy that followed the invasion, the civilian casualties, did anything to suppress Islamic terrorism.

Bolton's approach is tool thinking, in that it is not, in fact, about the actual issue at all and more about how to win an argument about the moral supremacy of the United States. History is not about how people feel; it cannot be appraised in neat algorithms. For example, the British introduced railways in India, but millions died in the Bengal famine. How many dead Indians equal a railway? How many Iraqi deaths is an unmistakable signal of power worth? How much political chaos, still roiling the country as I write these words, equals the value of accomplishing the military mission with "great speed"? This sort of equivocation turns history into a constantly evolving account with the purpose of erasing wrongdoing. "With or without actual WMD," Bolton wrote, Hussein was a security threat and his removal has made the world a safer place. In plain sight, Bolton moved the goalposts. There can be no acknowledgment of the mistakes made in Iraq because history in a political culture predicated on exceptionalism is a matter of loyalty, of propaganda rather than of fact. Correction does not have to end in self-flagellation though, merely recognition. It is only because history has been so warped and sewn into the fabric of identity that its refutation must come at the expense of that identity.

Another fallacy flows from balance sheet reasoning—that of contextualization—the idea that things were just different all the way back then. In defense of never removing monuments dedicated to slave owners and their defenders, professor of philosophy Gary Shapiro wrote in 2017 that "destroying or removing the structures eliminates opportunities for productively using our past. Critical contextualization is the better alternative."

This critical contextualization justification for not appraising historical characters and events in their full moral dimension is selective and, in many cases, just plain wrong. It assumes that at any given time there was a uniform and time-specific set of ethics. How change ever came about if this is true is a mystery. Those who say US slavery was just a feature of the times present slavery as a universally agreed practice, one around which there was no argument and no controversy, no opposition, no ethical protest and, in fact, no civil war. This ironically and inadvertently erases the efforts of those, both white and black, who pushed the moral panic button. Anti-slavery campaigners' efforts would go on to play much better in the story of America's exceptionalism than a fairy tale of cruelties that were visited with no ill intent or awareness because those were simply the values of that era. The "it was a different time" fallacy is used to excuse all sorts of bigotries, both in the past and in the current day. It takes for granted that there is always such total consensus around prejudice, that people just couldn't possibly have known that racism was wrong. It washes even less if applied in the present. A small-town homophobe or racist grandparent cannot claim ignorance: they are just choosing not to learn.

The same applies to the history of imperialism, whereby voices who spoke out against it within Britain are left out of the "contextualization" explanation. And of course, the erased voices of the enslaved and colonized themselves, who had a thing or two to say about their status and treatment. They have been omitted.

Greatness again, but only for the few

Gore Vidal once described his country as the United States of Amnesia. "We learn nothing because we remember nothing," he wrote. If I may paraphrase, we learn nothing because we remember only some things. I am keen, though, to stress that the solution to this cherry-picking of history and the way it informs present-day superiority complexes is not through engagement in another exercise of score settling. One of the dangers of the myth of a virtuous origin is that it drags everyone into balance-sheet thinking. History is not a story, despite that being implied by the very word. It is not a narrative, not a discussion, not a debate. It is a matter of facts. What is important is that they are presented, rather than relitigated.

All other approaches are dead ends. What is required is an addendum to the histories already written, as they have been captured in sculpture, popular culture, and education. What is required is the Berlin Topography approach. If there were an honest, fulsome education there would be no need for history to be contested via the medium of statues and op-eds by neocons. It is only because there is such a gap, such a vacuum of ignorance, that notions of nationalism and exceptional origin keep creeping into the realm of history. In 2013, when then prime minister of Britain David Cameron visited the site of the 1919 Amritsar massacre, where British Indian Army troops were ordered to open fire on a crowd of peaceful demonstrators, he expressed regret but no apology. Despite the outrage this caused, he stuck with his refusal to apologize. His approach illustrated the two different ways these accounts can be treated.

"I think the right thing is to acknowledge what happened, to recall what happened, to show respect and understanding for what happened." So far so good, but then Cameron went on to say: "That is why the words I used are right: to pay respect to those who lost their lives, to remember what happened, to learn the lessons, to reflect on the fact that those who were responsible were rightly criticized at the time, to learn from the bad and to cherish the good."

To learn from the bad and cherish the good. That is the myth of national exceptionalism, that the bad came with the good, and that the good really is the heart of a country's origin—a place that exists in the past, and which can be recaptured.

The United States is in the process of being cannibalized by an *again* that only ever applies to a certain demographic, a certain class. *Again* is about a return to exclusivity. That cultivation of nostalgia for the past is a dangerous thing, argues Rajiv Joseph, a US dramatist of Indian ancestry. To him, "Let's make America great again" really means, " 'Let's get back to being led by white males.' In the US, there's a certain nostalgia for the white male perspective, and the same it seems to me is true of films and TV about India. There's always going to be the perspective that those were the good old days. But, of course, they weren't."

6

The Myth of Gender Equality

*Revolutionary men with principles were not really different
from the rest. They used their cleverness to get, in return
for principles, what other men buy with their money.*

—*Nawal El Saadawi*

O f all those caught on the sharp end of mythmaking, none is
told as quickly and as impatiently that they are asking for too
much, for more than they deserve, than a woman who is asking
for her rights. The myth, or rather the con, is that in the West, we
have built a society in which women have secured gender equality—
maternity leave, marital choice, reproductive rights. Any inequality beyond these basic rights is just a function of biology. Any hope
for more is greedy, or simply misunderstanding the science. This is
thrown in the face of all calls for additional rights. All that can be
done has been done. How can you rewire biology?

The myth of gender equality deploys three arguments. The first
is *complementarity*, a sociobiological determinism which holds that
biology dictates social roles and behavior. The second is *progress*,
positing that any advances in women's rights at any point in time are

exhaustive. The third, *overcorrection*, scaremongers that women are destroying men by claiming sexual harassment and not following due process. These arguments are then reinforced by an argumentative tool I call *the setup*, a way of constantly killing the question for more rights by indulging in comparative deflection; are things not better today? Do you not see how others elsewhere are faring?

The social contract between the state and its female citizens is broken. This contract is a sort of bargain, where one gives up some rights voluntarily to create an order in which everyone can pursue individual happiness. Every day, women are giving up rights involuntarily to live in an order which is not optimized for the pursuit of their individual or collective happiness. It is not even optimized for their safety. As hard-won abortion rights in the US are rolled back, as the gender pay gap continues to persist and even widen, and as cybersexual harassment and online abuse become an everyday part of a woman's life, women are told not only that things are fine, but that they have in fact never been better. I was used to this logic, this myth of gender equality, but did not expect to see it spread in the boardrooms of London, the respectable media of Britain and the United States, and the polite society of ostensibly liberal circles in those two countries.

Growing up in a conservative family in the Middle East and North Africa, I was quick to learn of this system of bargaining, where the ultimate spoils were not happiness, but survival. Much of my life was conditional. My education in an English-language school was conditional on the fact that it did not Westernize me too much—the threat of being pulled out and enrolled in a religious school always hovered. Later, my professional chances were conditional on how many of my natural interests I could jettison in order to study for an appropriate career in medicine or its derivatives. My social status was conditional on my deportment—ideally a sort of demure but knowing fragility.

Cultivating this air was my biggest failure, a pose I could not strike no matter how hard I tried. I was scrappy, unkempt, in awe of my sisters and female relatives who glided through life, Sphinxlike, geisha-like, respected by the menfolk and orbited by other women. I could not, despite trying very hard, replace my chaotic natural temperament with a more gathered demeanor. I played too much soccer in the street with the neighborhood boys and experimented with eating or smoking quite a lot of what was growing wild and poisonous in the garden and surrounding brush. I remember at least two stomach-pumping incidents. I was constantly bruised and in trouble. My consistent failure to be the sort of daughter who shadows womenfolk in kitchens and salons frustrated my parents, who threw everything at the problem—religion, physical punishment, threats of being withdrawn from school.

For my father, who once told me "men are an ax, they break things; women are a bowl, they gather things," the problem was not that I could not be free to be who I was, but that I could not embrace the freedom that only my "natural" role in life could provide. The only way to find any peace was to accept the norms of a society that I did not understand nor saw any logic to, and to try to be really good at them. The only way was to give myself up and excel at performing, to pretend to be a bowl.

Complementarity

Complementarity is the belief that much of what women complain about cannot be legislated away because it's just human nature. The shrugging default to the rules of biology is universal across cultures—almost comfortingly so. To object to anything from forced marriage in Omdurman, Sudan, to the ubiquity of sexual harassment in the workplace in the City of London is to be met with this defense. And with it a demand that a woman makes the biggest trade-off of all—to accept that inequality is a function of biology. The only way to avoid the wild's reddened tooth and claw is never to step outside the bounds of nature's purdah. Biology is our destiny.

In Western societies, we can easily dismiss this determinism as backward when it is dictated by religion or by mullah-led governments in countries that are "other." But the very same fallacy runs the logic of female subordination everywhere. From New York to Tehran, women will be told that they are asking for it if they wear a short skirt in a bar or a looser-than-acceptable burqa in the street. The preachers of the myth that bad male behavior is inevitable and thus excusable if women provoke it aren't just restricted to religion. We have not made as much progress as we think. Sexual conservatism and slut-shaming—bizarrely wrapped up in a pornified culture—rigid heteronormativity and casual misogyny slapped me in the face when I settled in the UK, and they continue to surprise me to this day. The regressive gender roles that we think we have left behind as society has secularized are still present in academia and science. They are hiding in plain sight in popular culture and our social mores and they inform our political legislation.

And they are, if anything, getting more popular. In 2017, Jordan Peterson, a Canadian psychologist, became a best-selling author with his book *12 Rules for Life*. In this self-help manual for alienated men, Peterson dispenses advice that urges them to toughen up and for everyone to accept genetic order in a sort of happy existential oblivion that comes from knowing that "the pursuit of happiness is a pointless goal." It's almost Sufi-like. This ascetic Muslim sect seeks oneness with God and a higher state of spirituality in general by eschewing the material ambitions of brief earthly life and seeking transcendence in trance states of consciousness. Peterson's position on women is that because of their genetic makeup, they should not wander from their natural perch in the order. He attributes their modern distress at being torn between the demands of work and home to the fact that women went walkabout off the nature reserve.

According to Peterson, the gender pay gap, the average difference between the remuneration for men and women in employment—around 20 percent to the benefit of men in the US and the UK—is largely a natural reflection of existing differences between men and women. These differences are explained in his adaptation of the "Big Five personality traits" taxonomy: openness to experience, conscientiousness, extroversion, agreeableness, and neuroticism. Peterson is fixated on "agreeableness" in general, a classic fondness that conservative men have for women in what they perceive to be their natural state—fecund, comely, pliable. Other differences between the genders include "neuroticism," a woman's higher likelihood to experience stress, depression, and emotional volatility, and her need to be cooperative and compassionate. Women have preferences, one of which is to have less-demanding careers—or none at all. Social pressure forcing women to work in higher-paying jobs, or any job at all when they would like to remain at home, would actually work against their interests by interfering with their preferred choices. This is all underscored by another trope, that of "complementarity." Men are not superior to women, men are "complementary."

More than a century ago, British biologists Sir Patrick Geddes and Sir John Arthur Thomson made the same points—and managed to do so with a far more robust attempt at scientific method than Peterson. So much for progress. They argued that social, psychological, and behavioral traits were caused by the difference in metabolic state between men and women. Women supposedly conserve energy—by being "anabolic" —and this makes them passive, conservative, sluggish, stable, and uninterested in politics. Men expend their surplus energy by being "catabolic." This makes them eager, energetic, passionate, and variable, thereby interested in political and social matters.

It is rare that these pseudoscientific conclusions are just left at that. Often, these judgments justify a world where women should be subordinate. Peterson is often hailed as an innovator, a truth teller, when all he does is repeat and repackage ancient traditional gender role conservatism.

Geddes and Thomson's biological "facts" about metabolic states were used not only to explain behavioral differences between women and men but also to map out a path for social arrangements. These facts were used specifically to argue for withholding political rights from women because, Geddes and Thomson claimed, "what was decided among the prehistoric Protozoa cannot be annulled by Act of Parliament." And so, women cannot be granted political rights because they are not built for that purpose—and it would be pointless anyway, as women would not be interested in exercising them. And if they were forced, as Peterson argued more than 130 years later, it would traumatize them. There is a rich history of leveraging "science" and "facts" with the end of arguing that inequality is in fact hardwired.

In the 1970s, menstruation was used to argue that women should not become airline pilots since their monthly hormonal instability would render them unable to perform their duties as well as men—or at all. More recently, differences in male and female brains have been used to explain behavioral discrepancies. The anatomy of the corpus callosum, a knot of nerves that connects the two hemispheres of the brain, was studied for a 1992 article in *Time* magazine. The article surveyed then popular biological explanations of differences between women and men, claiming that women's thicker corpora callosa could explain "women's intuition" and what impairs women's ability to perform some specialized visuospatial skills, such as map reading. A woman cannot have an advantage over a man biologically without it counting against her in some other way, you see. Her "intuition" must be at the cost of her motor skills. Even a woman who is a disembodied bundle of nerves on a laboratory slab is forced into a trade-off.

Scientific biological determinism has a tendency to reach for the comforting takeaway that we can blame it all on wiring and go home. In 2013, clinical psychologist Simon Baron-Cohen opened his book *The Essential Difference* with the hard assertion that "the female brain is predominantly hardwired for empathy. The male brain is predominantly hardwired for understanding and building systems." But he dilutes this later in the work by saying that one doesn't have to be a man to have a male brain or a woman to have a female brain, which surely is the whole point of his thesis.

In a later study led by Baron-Cohen in 2018, one claiming to be the largest-ever analysis of the relationship between psychological sex differences and autistic traits, there are more smoke-and-mirror displays. Part of the study involved calculating the difference (or "D-score") between each individual's score on tests of systemizing (understanding rule-based systems) and empathy. According to the study report, in the typical population, men, on average, tended toward a high D-score, meaning they engage in more systemizing than empathy, whereas women, on average, tended toward a low D-score, meaning they went the opposite way. The research got its headlines. "Men and Women Really Do Think Differently, Say Scientists," ran the *Times* of London. "The much-maligned but long-standing idea that women enjoy discussing their emotions while men are mostly excited by cars may be true after all."

The *New Statesman* published a closer inspection of the study by professor of neuroimaging Gina Rippon, however, and it emerged that the study report had actually said that individual "differences in empathising and systemising account for nineteen times more of the variance in autistic traits than other measures, such as sex." In other words, despite what it reported about some general gender-based traits, the study actually concluded that a high individual D-score is a better predictor of autism than whether one is male. This key data point was ignored in publicity about the study in favor of a reductive view that boiled all such differences down to gender, and not to the difference between empathizing and systemizing in a given individual. So strong are the political and social motivations to label brains pink and blue that we end up with what Rippon calls "neurotrash." In her 2019 book *The Gendered Brain: The New Neuroscience That Shatters the Myth of the Female Brain*, she calls these persistent attempts to gender brains at the expense of women "Whac-a-Mole" myths. They keep turning up no matter how many times they are debunked.

It is one of the most persistent deflections, this justification of the way things are by looking for biological or genetic smoking guns. Biological determinism discounts bad male behavior and chastises women for demanding better. And it is promoted by people who would never think of themselves as having a regressive view of the world.

In November 2017, after the Harvey Weinstein scandal broke, the premier BBC news program, *Newsnight*, held a debate on sexual harassment, calling it "The problem with men." It began with host Evan Davis, the first openly gay presenter of the show and a liberal with an ear piercing, standing in a zoo. As he walked past the cages he asked if sexual harassment was part of our biology, like the impulses of the animals behind him? The ensuing panel conversation featured fourteen angry men and three bewildered women. It immediately careened into the territory of men expressing frustration that in this new world, natural dynamics where women are touched against their will are now being policed.

A deluge of responses to the #MeToo movement fell along these lines—that of biology being pushed up against the wall by a feminist movement drunk with power. Pundits, columnists, and academics listened to stories of women being touched, professionally intimidated by requests for sexual favors, and even assaulted, and responded with a collective outcry against what they perceived was a violation of the benign status quo. Men must woo women in order to procreate and in that melee, sometimes things just get a little messy.

In the UK, the author Douglas Murray concluded that #MeToo, if allowed to grow unchecked, augured the end of the human race. Writing in the *Spectator* magazine he catastrophized: "The rules are being redrawn with little idea of where the boundaries of this new sexual utopia will lie and less idea still of whether any sex will be allowed in the end." The journalist Peter Hitchens went down the creative route of concluding that all that women gain from this "squawking" about sex pests is that they will be forced to wear a niqab. Other journalists helpfully weighed in. Giles Coren in the *Times* of London expressed ironically resigned confusion about how one is to navigate this scary new world without accidentally sexually assaulting someone. Rod Liddle, a man cautioned for kicking his pregnant girlfriend in the stomach, wondered if women are just hardwired to be attracted to powerful men. Brendan O'Neill of online magazine *Spiked* called #MeToo a "sexual inquisition," saying it was a "sinister menace to democracy." The former *Guardian* journalist Michael White went on BBC radio to call Westminster female reporters, who had overcome years of self-doubt to step forward and accuse male Members of Parliament of touching them inappropriately, "predators." Bret Stephens of the *New York Times* concluded that it had all already gone too far, appealing for nuance between rape and other forms of sexual assault—a conflation no one was making. It was a corporeal spasm.

These are not reactionaries, provocateurs, or trolls. They are mainstream journalists across the political divide. What they are exhibiting is a typical response to the challenging of a deep-seated myth, that biology is destiny, by resorting to deflection and hyperbole. If we are going to stick with the obsessive commitment to biology as explainer for all behavior, a helpful way to look at this phenomenon would be to see these people less as thinking individuals with agency, but more as organisms on top of a food chain reacting with instinctive self-preservation to what they perceive to be an existential threat. Judge by biology always, and you will be judged by it inevitably.

The Tool—The Setup

En masse, anti-#MeToo voices represent strong cultural resistance to a counter narrative, no matter how obvious the claim or credible the source. In 2014, UN special rapporteur Rashida Manjoo said that sexism in the UK is more "in your face" and generally worse than in other countries that she has visited. The response was a howl of denial, protesting that the UK had come a long way, and that it was absurd to compare it to countries where women suffer female genital mutilation or forced marriage. But Manjoo had not compared the UK to Somalia or Saudi Arabia. She had made a rather obvious statement that described the pervasive "old boys" network in the UK, and the aggressiveness and ubiquity of commercial sexualized depictions of women. She also said that "violence against women needs to be addressed within the broader struggles against inequality and gender-based discrimination."

More revealing was how the debate was then framed. Rather than engaging with what Manjoo said, which was anodyne and generic, the conversation became a comparative one. Was Britain better or worse than other countries? Was Britain better or worse than before with regard to gender equality? The answers could obviously only be that of course Britain was better than other countries and better than before. It was a setup. The setup tool is an argumentative device that distracts from discussing the issue at hand by diverting attention to something unrelated. Once its methods are identified, the pattern is obvious.

A statement about sexist culture in the UK by Manjoo, a gender expert diplomat, is rebuffed by the worthy banality that at least women's genitals are safe from mutilation on its green and pleasant land. An attempt to have a discussion about the culture of violence against women becomes one about how safe they are compared to other countries. An attempt to understand why rapes in London rose by 20 percent in 2017 becomes a conversation about the semantics of the statistics. Maybe incidents of rape have not gone up at all but they're just being reported more? Or what if, in fact, all crime has gone up, not just rape?

It could be worse. It has been worse. And in fact, it is worse elsewhere. On a macro level, trying to have a meaningful excavation of sexual abuse and assault is like presenting in serious pain to a physician who immediately asks you to consider that at least you are not dead. The point of the setups is to avoid engaging with the primary malady while maintaining the moral high ground. It is far easier to filibuster on why rape reports are rising than it is to say, simply, that you do not care about rape.

These setups develop, like sentient straw men defensively scrambling to prevent any real discussion, in order to preserve the way things are. A system of inequality must create its own illusion of justice, through which it is sustained. It is a common impulse, not unique to any culture. Setups are stabilizers, low-key propaganda that things simply are not that bad. The starker and more graphic the injustice, the louder and more feverishly it is normalized and excused.

Progress—But Look How Far We've Come

The argument of progress can be used to mask the fact that advances are always relative, rarely absolute. Just because things were worse yesterday does not mean that they are ideal today or should not be improved upon. The argument also ignores the reproduction of social and cultural norms that continue to hold women back. When any complaint can be dismissed as ungratefulness, it is impossible to secure any further wins.

The first response for a demand for more rights is to look back and remonstrate, almost implicitly threaten, that it could all be so much worse. It is a reflex deployed against women's rights activists throughout history. It is also an impulse that we can easily shed when judging other societies, dropping relativist perspectives. Few Westerners would look at Saudi Arabia and observe that where the country is now with women's rights is fine, considering women were only allowed an education fifty years ago. But they might smugly think that advancement in their own countries is satisfactory, without considering that the most basic political right, that of universal suffrage, was granted in the United States and United Kingdom less than one hundred years ago. In Switzerland, women's suffrage was only granted in 1971. It is also easier to acknowledge toxicity in a culture that isn't our own. The murder of women by members of their family in Pakistan or Jordan is easily identified as an honor killing and traced back to deeply ingrained religious, social, and cultural norms that see women's lives as owned by their families in general, and by their male relatives in particular. The same line of reasoning is not made when considering the fact that in the US, three women a day are killed by their partners or ex-partners and that half of all homicides in the country are committed by an intimate partner. According to the World Health Organization, the global figure is high but still less than in the United States, hovering around 38 percent of homicide cases. In England and Wales, in the first half of this decade, 64 percent of all women killed by men were murdered by their partners or ex-partners. An entire project in the UK, *Counting Dead Women*, collated by Women's Aid and feminist researcher Karen Ingala Smith, was founded in 2012 because no official authority was making the gender link. If these are not considered honor killings, then no uncomfortable examination needs to be conducted into what lies beneath. But they are honor killings, in that they are committed in order to avenge a slight to a man and restore the honor that a woman's disobedient behavior has taken away, because a woman is the property of her partner. The only difference between Western and Eastern honor killings is that the latter are sometimes perpetrated by extended male family members and sometimes mothers, but all that tells us is that in Western societies a woman's ownership has been transferred from her family to her male partner.

In general, invoking progress is irrelevant when discussing serious, systemic female disempowerment or cultural failures to protect women from violence. Malcolm X, faced with his own version of the progress roadblock in the race debate—where the argument was that African Americans were not being lynched anymore—said: "If you stick a knife in my back nine inches and pull it out six inches, there's no progress. If you pull it all the way out that's not progress. Progress is healing the wound that the blow made. And they haven't even pulled the knife out much less heal the wound."

Backsliding

The fixation with progress overlooks the real danger of backsliding. When Donald Trump took office, he revoked the 2014 Fair Pay and Safe Workplaces Executive Order, which, among other "violations," withheld taxpayer dollars from companies that did not provide paycheck transparency and prohibited forced arbitration clauses that effectively barred cases from going to court for sexual harassment, sexual assault, or discrimination claims. The Trump administration also reversed a directive that forced colleges to quickly investigate on-campus sexual assault. President Barack Obama had enacted the requirement, which lowered the burden of proof and cut federal funding if schools weren't compliant, in 2011. Trump also rolled back an Obamacare provision requiring employers to offer health insurance that covered birth control. He signed a law that lets local governments withhold federal funding from healthcare providers like Planned Parenthood that offer abortions along with a number of other women's healthcare treatments like breast cancer screenings. One month later he proposed a federal budget that defunded Planned Parenthood—which is already barred from using federal funds for abortion services in most cases—completely. In the period since Trump came to office and June 2019, according to the Guttmacher Institute, twenty-seven abortion bans were enacted across twelve states, with more in the legislation pipeline. This rollback initiative does not only affect the United States. Immediately after his inauguration, Trump also instituted the Mexico City policy, more accurately known as the "global gag rule" that makes nongovernmental organizations receiving US funds for global health issues prove they do not use their other funding to provide abortions or talk about the option with patients. NGOs could not use US aid for abortion services before this rule. Trump also stopped an Obama-crafted rule from going into effect that would make companies track payment data based on race and gender. The data was meant to help close the gender pay gap.

On a global level, according to the 2017 World Economic Forum (WEF) report on gender equality, there was a similar slowing down of positive trends. In that year progress toward gender parity shifted into reverse.

Now in its fourteenth year, the Global Gender Gap Report has given the WEF an opportunity to identify long-term trends in gender equality, and the picture that is emerging shows that there is a sort of terminal velocity that has been reached. The global gender gap measures four overall areas of inequality between men and women—economic participation and opportunity, educational attainment, political empowerment, and health and survival. While the global gender gap has narrowed since 2006, it has done so at a glacial pace. In 2020, that year's Global Gender Gap Report headlined its findings with the statement, "None of us will see gender parity in our lifetimes, and nor likely will many of our children." According to the report, at the current rate of progress, it will take another one hundred years for the world's women to be on an even footing with men. So even if one were to cite inexorable improvement in the world's only superpower and the land of the free, and in aggregate on a global basis, it would appear that progress does not have its own momentum. It is not fueled by the principles of the Enlightenment and oiled by the invisible hand of capitalism. It is a tentative and fragile state which is sustained by the effort of constant activism and vigilance, both on the ground and on the ideological battlefield. An appeal for context, to point out that the overall pattern is one of improvement, is an appeal for quietism.

And the complacency of progress does not account for the reactionary backlash that progress often triggers, which makes it doubly difficult for the dermal layer to be treated, for "the wound to heal."

Overcorrection—Has Feminism Gone Too Far?

All myths assume challenges are overcorrections, but when it comes to feminism, the "going too far" accusation has been the most consistent and aggressive barrier to equality. Overcorrection is the assumption that feminism will guilt society into creating another system of unfairness, one which will steal from the industrious and deserving rich (men) to give to the feckless poor (women). Ironically, implicit in this response is the concession that a correction does need to be made. The system is so skewed in one party's favor that if there is an opening for change there is a risk of a deluge.

"Has feminism gone too far?" is now a fixture in popular discourse. In 2018, a Sky poll on the question showed that 67 percent of Britons thought feminism had gone too far or should not go any further. It's a point that has—very much like "progress"—been present at every stage of the history of gender activism. It seems that no matter how much or how little feminism achieves, there will always be someone poised to ask if things aren't already going too far. It is less about what is achieved and more about the perception. Feminism has been going too far from the very moment the first woman asked for a basic right that a man had been afforded by birth.

The question has not even been reframed over the decades; it hangs crude and unrefined by events or changes in popular culture, rebuking gender activism, scaling back ambition, and stigmatizing progress. The question alone and its persistence reflects the low point we are always starting from, the suspicion of gender equality as a gateway for something else, something sinister, something that will disturb the natural order.

In a 1994 PBS episode of *Think Tank* entitled—you guessed it—"Has Feminism Gone Too Far?" two feminist writers made the argument that feminism, or at least what they perceived to be the wrong type of feminism, has gone too far. They make the distinction between their school of equity feminism—that which seeks technical equality for women in civil, legal, and professional matters—and the "too far" school of "gender feminism"—which aims to eliminate gender roles altogether. The interview is more than twenty years old but could have been aired today, so much does it chime with contemporary themes: accusations of ingratitude for how good things already are, trivializing of complaint as indulgence; even campus moral outrages and the pathetic victim culture of students. One of the guests, Christina Hoff Sommers, whose books include *Who Stole Feminism?*, said: "No women have ever had more opportunities, more freedom, and more equality than contemporary American women. And at that moment the movement becomes more bitter and more angry. Why are they so angry?" She then went on to say that feminism had become "a kind of totalitarianism. Many young women on campuses combine two very dangerous things: moral fervor and misinformation. On the campuses they're fed a kind of catechism of oppression."

Change is not constant, but resistance to it is. The vitriol expressed by Sommers and her co-guest Camille Paglia, also an academic and writer—described as being the "spokeswoman for the anti-feminist backlash"—toward their generation's cohort of feminist activists ages very well. Here they speak about Anita Hill, an attorney who in 1991 testified before the Senate Judiciary Committee as part of Clarence Thomas's Supreme Court nomination process. She gave detailed statements accusing him of sexual harassment. The Senate still went on to confirm Thomas to the Supreme Court.

Paglia boasted that "I was the only leading feminist that went out against Anita Hill. I think that that whole case was a pile of crap. I think it was absurd. First of all, again, a totalitarian regime, OK, is where ten years after the fact you're nominated now for a top position in your country and you are being asked to reconstruct lunch conversations that you had with someone who never uttered a peep. OK? This is to Anita Hill: 'All right, when he started to talk again about this [*sic*] pornographic films at lunch in the government cafeteria, what did you do?' 'I tried to change the subject.' Excuse me! I mean, that is ridiculous. I mean, so many of these cases . . ."

Sommers chimes in: "He never touched her . . . he never touched her."

"He never touched her, OK?" Paglia seethes. "That was such a trumped-up case by the feminist establishment."

Little has changed since then. When Christine Blasey Ford brought sexual assault allegations against Bret Kavanaugh more than a quarter century after Anita Hill's testimony against Clarence Thomas, the similarity in the attacks leveled at both women to discredit them was chilling. In some instances, the attacks were leveled by the same people who had made them twenty-seven years earlier. Senators Chuck Grassley of Iowa and Orrin G. Hatch of Utah, both Republicans, were on the Judiciary Committee during both the Thomas and Kavanaugh sexual assault investigations. Hatch had said of Anita Hill that her account seemed "too contrived, too slick." Blasey Ford's account was not sufficiently slick for him. He said she sounded "mixed up" and might have confused Kavanaugh with someone else.

The 1995 PBS episode and the smear campaigns against Hill and Ford feature evergreen tropes. Harping on about sexual harassment as not "rape-rape," they say, teaches a lack of agency because it puts all the blame on men for their transgressions, be they verbal or physical, and not on women for failing to enforce boundaries. Male transgression is just a matter of bad wiring—they simply weren't told often enough that what they were doing is bad. This is a serious misreading of how male entitlement works and how often boundary-setting not only fails to discourage offensive behavior but inflames it. In a US publication, *When Men Murder Women—An Analysis of 2015 Homicide Data*, it was determined that 68 percent of women murdered by intimate partners or ex-partners were targeted because of a rejection or a challenge.

Another ancient theme is that moral frenzy is encroaching upon justice and tainting bewildered good men. Due process is at risk because once a woman makes an accusation, a man is assumed guilty. This is a dogged belief that is indifferent to two realities: low conviction rates of men accused of sexual assault, and lack of social censure of men convicted of sexual assault. Neither of these suggest a society in a hurry to lock men up or shun them for sexual offenses. A study by the University of Chicago found that in the US, Australia, Canada, England, Wales, and Scotland, only 7 percent of cases resulted in a conviction for the original offense charged—and only 13 percent led to a conviction of any sexual offense, despite there being a rise in reporting of such crimes. The main reason cited for this was attrition; the cases just lost steam before they came to court because women were intimidated, were not given enough support, or were legally left exposed by corroboration burdens that render victim statements alone—for a crime that usually occurs in private—insufficient. Due process for men is healthy and thriving.

Social censure seems also not to have been overly aggressive if one takes into consideration how powerful men such as film director Roman Polanski are still celebrated, despite the fact that a 1977 charge of sexual assault for the rape of a thirteen-year-old girl in the United States has still not been prosecuted because Polanski fled the country. Professionally, there are other high-profile cases where moral fervor would be expected to take over but has not. At the height of the #MeToo outpouring of pent-up accusations, Glenn Thrush, a senior White House correspondent at the *New York Times*, was accused of making unwelcome passes at female colleagues in a previous role and then, when rejected, taking a playground revenge by making up details of sexual encounters to his male colleagues that cast him in a desirable, flattering light at the expense of the women who spurned him. After a careful investigation the newspaper decided that he had behaved in a way that made his female colleagues feel professionally compromised. He was censured but not fired. Brett Kavanaugh, accused of sexual assault when he was a teenager, was questioned, vetted, and then confirmed as a Supreme Court justice. If lack of "due process" means that we are beginning to redefine inappropriate sexual behavior outside of the brutally coercive, this is not failing men, it is having a long-overdue reckoning.

The overcorrection argument works to trivialize women's grievances, either by disbelieving them or disrespecting them because they're pathetic. It paints women as both a sort of knowing lobby and a wretched helpless class of tattletales who cannot handle their business. Women are somehow both canny, steely agents of a grievance industry, secretly shaking hands as they step into the vista of flashing camera lights on their way to smear your man, and also limp, passive, and suffering due to their learned victimhood. They are either manipulative or inviting of assault by not being assertive enough.

Who Are the Allies?

I wanted to end this book on the myth of gender equality because it illustrates an important point—the enemies of change are not always obvious. Whether it is political correctness, freedom of speech, or the whitewashing of history, these ideas are held widely in society and cut across political orientation, gender, and race. That's what makes them so insidious. The myth of gender equality isn't just propped up by cartoonish bad men who hoard the spoils of patriarchy. It's held dearly by the "good" men as well. The woke brothers, the "I'm on your side" dudes, the "I'm a father to daughters and I'm appalled" dads. This good man doesn't quite exist in pure ally form, he is an apparition summoned to stall a deeper appraisal of gender dynamics by classifying men into good and bad. They are either alleyway rapists or they are well-meaning flirts—there is nothing in between.

But what is a "good man"? Is it Eric Schneiderman, a former New York attorney general, a Democrat, and a man who has raised his voice against sexual misconduct and who has been accused by four women of physical violence and abuse? Or is it Mike Pence, the monogamous, religious vice president, who will not be alone in a room with a woman other than his wife, but who supported the Trump administration's dismantling of Obama-era gender discrimination laws? There is no obvious partition between good and bad men, and certainly none that can be traced along ideological, religious, or political lines.

The list of high-profile sexual abuse accusations continues to grow, and it is populated equally by liberals and conservatives. From Charlie Rose and Matt Lauer to Roger Ailes and Bill O'Reilly, misogyny has no politics, ideology, or religion. It is why we constantly fail to make the connection between male violence and any cultural or social norms that give men a sense of entitlement over women and their sexual compliance, the "honor killings" that are so easily identifiable in other cultures. When a man "snaps," and murders his partner and/or his children, it is seen as an unfortunate individual malfunction. A 2015 Birmingham University study in the UK, which compared reporting on domestic violence in the *Guardian* and the *Sun*, found that even though the two British papers were different in their political orientation and target audience, they both were guilty of reporting crime by way of its trigger—that is—the female victim:

> *Unless the man is framed as a "monster," the focus is on the woman (either leaving or staying) rather than the perpetrator. There are some interesting exceptions to this, for example, where the woman is the perpetrator of the violence, she is the main focus of the article. Another exception is when the domestic violence perpetrator is a well-known person, as in much of the articles on celebrities—in these articles there is relatively little attention for their victim.*

The study also found that many articles mention issues that "can be seen to reduce the blame of the male perpetrator—for example, alcohol, football results, depression, lack of employment, or the women's behavior." It also cited articles which suggested that jury prejudice is one reason why so few men are convicted for rape and domestic violence, due to the belief that there may be some aspect of female culpability. In both the *Guardian* and the *Sun*, reporters made the point that many abusers have been maltreated in their childhood. Raising such issues suggests that they "explain" why men are violent toward their partners, and they infer that there's no further need to search for the reasons behind that violence or what can be done to prevent it. Female victims of male violence are, largely, presented as those who have been punished for failing to keep up their part of the women's bargain—in this instance, behaving or dressing in ways provocative to men.

An entire online subculture has been built on the notion of "involuntary celibacy," the inability to find a romantic partner despite desiring one. Incels—involuntary celibates—blame women for rejecting them and for radicalizing them to seek revenge through violence. At least four proven cases of murder in North America have referenced involuntary celibacy as a motivation or have referenced incel culture, including the February 2018 Marjory Stoneman Douglas High School shootings in Florida. But the ensuing analysis is still about the "redistribution of sex" rather than the entitlement to it.

Misogyny has no track record and is easily divisible from the rest of a man's behavior. The "good men" trope also fails to account for all the ways change is resisted by men who would never physically or sexually abuse a woman, men who are au fait with the boundaries of verbal transgression and would recognize even coercive control as a form of abuse. In her book *Why So Slow?*, Virginia Valian found that while men can embrace the need for efforts that lead to fairness, such as equal pay, they have a much harder time with their own loss of centrality. To these men, the end of the patriarchy is actually the end of the world.

In her essay "MIA: The Liberal Men We Love," Professor Amy Butcher writes about the wall erected by the good men. In a post-Trump world, she observes how men have begun to appear in a different light to their female partners, friends, and siblings who assumed they were on the right side of the sexism debate. She writes a dispatch from the world of liberal women bewildered by men "previously, pleasantly, progressive—rising up with unprecedented hos-

tility, anger, abandon, and resentment." The reason for their transformation is female anger at Trump's election, his normalization of
sexual assault and verbal degradation of women. To the men it was
too much, too strident, too shrill. It was just "locker room talk." The
pushback began as a minimization of Trump's language and alleged
sexual transgressions and developed into something altogether
more sinister:

> *These are, make no mistake, men who wholly sought us for our
> strength, our independence and education. The jobs we held or
> coveted. The degrees degreed in our name. Our passions and
> pursuits and our can-do, want-it-all attitudes. They work as
> medical researchers or in the arts, in teaching or social work.
> They queue up the* Saturday Night Live *skits that humiliate
> Trump, to consume with our coffee on Sunday mornings, but
> find it unpalatable and unpleasant that our resentment and our
> fears linger long into the workweek.*

She reported on men who burned their wives' Women's March
T-shirts and Hillary Clinton paraphernalia. Men who left their partners because they could no longer tolerate their anger. Men who
scolded their wives for teaching their daughters bad manners.

To some men, a woman's right to be a victim can be a scary
thing because it implies that the next stage is retribution and, then
simply, change. In a 1980 paper entitled "Why Men Resist," sociol-
ogist William J. Goode ascribed their behavior to the natural self-
preservation instinct of any dominant group.

"Men view even small losses of deference, advantages, or opportunities as large threats and losses," he wrote. "Their own gains, or

their maintenance of old advantages, are not noticed as much. Since any given cohort of men knows they did not create the system that gives them their advantages, they reject any charges that they conspired to dominate women."

If a man believes that 81 percent of women have experienced sexual harassment since their teenage years, then it means he must examine his own behavior and that of his male friends and colleagues. He must conduct an exercise of self-reflection on the part of his gender and take responsibility for changing a system he had no hand in creating. This is uncomfortable. And it is a lot of work to do for no material or immediate gain.

So, a woman's victimhood is rejected. Ironically, this is where denial of agency happens. It takes agency to be a victim; it takes grit, determination, confidence, and honesty to stop running away from pain and perceived humiliation, to assert that you have been compromised professionally or physically for being a woman, and to reject the blame for that. Gritting teeth and moving on is not displaying agency.

And the good men who fail to acknowledge a woman's right to anger? Their instincts are right. They know that once a violation is validated, it paves the way for anger, for redress, and for expanding the definition of a woman's right. Validating anger is a gateway to the erosion of male equity. Butcher likens the sense of mission creep to a spider. It is "fast and without reproach. First the problem is on the porch. Then it is climbing up your bedpost. Look as it spins a web around your morning and then your month and then your marriage. Look—and please keep looking—as it grips and continues gripping everything you once held dear inside his web."

These men, warily seeing the spider approach, will not hesitate to use the artificial division between good and bad men to preserve their status and avoid criticism by claiming that none of this is their doing because you know what, they're the good guy. So, they recuse themselves from the discourse because women are just so angry all the time and it's not their fault. Call it "waving the good guy card."

But it is not always about fear of status loss, it is often because "good" men struggle with the perception of systemic bias, and even when they do not, they struggle with the notion that systemic bias can be corrected without creating a world that is unjust to men. They suffer from privilege blindness. This is not a quality that is unique to men as male, but to all who have enjoyed privilege while confusing it with fairness. There is something particularly elusive about the acknowledgment of female victimization. It is easy to see and empathize with the troubles of the poor and disenfranchised. To a lesser extent, it is also relatively easy to acknowledge that there is a higher degree of cruelty toward and exclusion of immigrants, people of color, or a specific group such as Muslims. A rational, "good" man can merely survey his own workplace and his nation's political institutions, media, and elite and come to the conclusion that there is infrastructural bias against the working class or racial minorities, as so few of them are visible in numbers.

Women, on the other hand, are everywhere. They are not in purdah. They are openly competing with men for places in schools and jobs. They are interviewing men and managing them and giving them a hard time. They are jostling with them in public spaces and lines, they are swiping the last of their favorite sandwiches from under their noses at the deli. Women's emotional pain is intangible, their physical pain inflicted behind closed doors—their compromised career prospects easily explained away by their childbearing and rearing responsibilities. Good men are capable of acknowledging and empathizing with individual relatable pain—that of their daughters, sisters, and female friends. But the connection between that and a society-wide issue is harder to make.

The good man is not the one who has sexually harassed his female colleague or hired a man instead of a woman specifically for gender reasons. As far as he is aware, he has never received overt preferential treatment for being a male. Why then must he or his son lose out on a place at school or work because it has been earmarked for a female in order to redress a diffuse gender grievance? Why must he pay higher taxes to fund childcare from which women will earn the greatest benefit? Why must he now be more mindful of how he behaves around women in case he comes across as sexually intimidating? Why must he pay reparations for individual crimes that he did not commit?

In the eyes of good men, women have demanded group punishment for individual miscarriages—a collective land grab from the innocent. This unsympathetic position is not evidence that feminism has gone too far and alienated even progressive men, but proof of how much work there is still to do both to make the connection between the personal and the endemic and, in turn, make the case that a system that is unfair to women results in its own injustices to men. The fate of good men and women, too often separated, is intertwined on both a practical and cultural level. Yet the framing of women's rights causes in popular mythology as shrill, entitled, and unnatural hides the organic and spontaneous advantages to men who, on the most basic level, stand to benefit.

In 2015, Pew-funded research in the US revealed that fathers were as likely as mothers to say that parenting was extremely important to their identity—57 percent of men and 58 percent of women. It also emerged that around 48 percent of fathers felt they were not doing enough childcare. Similar research, two years before, found that working fathers were as likely as working mothers to say they preferred to be at home with their children but failed to do so because of financial burdens. These are burdens that women cannot share equally because of compromised career prospects and expensive unsubsidized childcare.

Despite this obvious weight that men wish they could share with women, feminism is perpetually presented as misandry, further alienating the "good men." This is one of the evergreen responses to calls for female empowerment, along with the claim that feminism is some sort of grievance gravy train. But it has been given new life with a politicization of feminism as part of a reassertion of hierarchical, patriarchal order. In early 2018, a *Washington Post* survey by Ishaan Tharoor traced the centering of anti-feminist views in political rhetoric in Turkey, the United States, Russia, and the Philippines. There was a pattern: "Right-wing governments all wielding anti-feminism as a political cudgel. The enduring reality of the moment is that it remains a profoundly effective tactic."

A new orthodoxy

Women are often accused of wanting to throw the good out with the bad, of not knowing when to stop. But gender equality is a radical movement, it isn't asking for tinkering, it is asking for the correction of the patriarchy's fundamental structural imbalances. And so yes, what is required is, indeed, a new orthodoxy. What is required is, yes, even more policing of cultures that do not stigmatize bad male behavior. What is required is, in fact, narrowing down consent to its most unequivocal. These are not radical notions. The fear that they are radical has been instilled by all the arguments that come together to drain the present situation of its urgency.

This urgency is underscored by a resurgence in biological determinism and a backlash against attempts to widen the definition of gender jeopardy to include the wielding of male sexual power against subordinate women. But we end with the myth of gender equality because out of all the pervasive complacencies, it is the one that has, at the time of writing in 2020, despite a cultural backlash, witnessed a moment where reality caught up. It was brief. But action was taken to seek protection and redress for women who had been sexually compromised in the workplace by powerful men. The move toward justice happened slowly and cumulatively, via the compounded effort of women who refused to believe that the sanctity of their bodies should be traded for their professional success, those who refused to be grateful, and those who did not accept the stale logic of biology.

Conclusion

No one knows what a more democratic and inclusive culture would be like. It is fatuously omniscient to assume it
would be worse than what we already have. The attempt
of reactionaries to shut people down shows both fear and
stupidity. But it's too late: they will be hearing from us.

—Hanif Kureishi

The Boomerang Effect—Myths Are Bad for Everyone

Myths consume their believers.

The success of a myth depends on how well it can convince
enough people that they are exempt from its consequences. A myth
creates winners and losers, and then convinces its adherents that
they are the winners. Patriarchy continues to thrive because enough
men believe that they are winning, despite the system exerting such
pressures on them that in the United States men are 3.5 times more
likely to die by suicide than women.

The men convicted for assault or murder of a female partner are not winning; the boys emptying semiautomatics in their high schools because they were rejected by girls are not winning; the collateral damage—the children, the innocent bystanders, their murdered partners—are not winning. The myth of gender equality does not only deny the pain of women, it denies that of men.

The same can be said of all the other myths, they boomerang inevitably. One of Donald Trump's signature election promises was to build a wall along the US border with Mexico and that Mexico would pay for it. Once that promise clashed with reality and Trump demanded that the wall be paid for by the US taxpayer, he triggered the longest government shutdown in the history of the United States. His policies hit those who had voted for him to inflict the pain on others. A prison secretary affected by the shutdown interviewed by the *New York Times* in January 2019 put it very well when she said: "I voted for him, and he's the one who's doing this. I thought he was going to do good things. He's not hurting the people he needs to be hurting." He's not hurting the people he needs to be hurting. That in a nutshell is the boomerang effect of the myth. If a political program is based on empowering its supporters by appealing to their sense of superiority over the marginalized, it will come for its own believers at some point.

Trashing the culture of political correctness only creates a world where everyone's sensitivities are trampled upon. Trump voters have a taste for his insults because they were sick of a political correctness that coddled the feelings of those lower down the food chain. But these voters then had to contend with a president who is not saving his non-PC "honesty" just for Mexican immigrants or Muslims, but has extended it to disabled people, war heroes (John McCain, a "dummy"), the Supreme Court ("a mess"), his own Republican Party ("stupid"), the FBI, the CIA, US allies all over the world, and various politicians and media personalities, to whom he refers in terms of their physical or intellectual capabilities. "Like a dog" is one of his favorite insults. An immediate result was that in 2016, even before he became president, playground bullying mimicking Trump's humiliation tactics surged in American schools. Students picked up the frequency that Trump's comments transmitted. The SPLC gave the phenomenon a name, "The Trump Effect."

Similarly, free speech absolutism creates a race to the bottom by enabling the commodification of the spectacle of abuse and harassment. When conspiracy theorist Alex Jones was kicked off digital platforms for suggesting that the Sandy Hook massacre was fabricated—among other theories—he asked, "Now, who will stand against Tyranny and who will stand for free speech?" Shortly after, a defamation suit was brought against him—one of many—and he cited the First Amendment in his defense. When the court concluded that his free speech rights were not being violated because there should be an effort to balance "freedom of expression with the safeguarding of people's reputations," liberal free speech advocates were not convinced. On his talk show, Bill Maher indignantly said: "We're losing the thread, of the concepts that are important to this country. . . . Either you care about the real American shit or you don't. I don't like Alex Jones, but Alex Jones gets to speak."

How did we get here? To a place where a man like Alex Jones can make a career out of harassing the parents of children shot to death in school massacres, and this strange strain of free speech masochism still supports him? We are here because the lives the free speech crisis myth targets—the minorities, the women, the transgender high school students, the queers—are not sacred. And so now the myth's tentacles extend to defending abuse of grieving parents of slain schoolchildren. Once free speech becomes the absolute right to denigrate, it corrodes sensitivity to everyone. In his book *The Harm in Hate Speech*, professor of law and philosophy Jeremy Waldron spells out this blowback theory. The very point of hate speech, he says, "is to negate the implicit assurance that a society offers to the members of vulnerable groups—that they are accepted . . . as a matter of course, along with everyone else." Purveyors of hate "aim to undermine this assurance, call it in question, and taint it with visible expressions of hatred, exclusion and contempt." It would seem that the free speech "slippery slope" doesn't curve toward more curtailment of speech, but toward more license for speech in a way that makes everyone vulnerable to abuse, hatred, and by extension, violence.

In addition to privileging speech over dignity, free speech absolutism today just creates a toxic atmosphere for everyone, a wider cultural corruption. The popularization of abusing human beings for whatever end—ideological, personal, or just cynical—is the real free speech crisis. The exploitation of free speech to set up "roll up, roll up!" circus performances is contributing to an extremism that is lucrative for everyone, from the BBC and CNN to Alex Jones.

On a large scale, these emissions can pollute the environment, sometimes literally. Climate change deniers are invited to push "facts" that are nothing but opinions and are given the imprimatur of truth and legitimacy by virtue of appearing on large and respectable platforms. In a matter of months after the coronavirus pandemic started, wearing a face mask became not about slowing the spread of a deadly disease, but about the freedom to refuse to wear one, about rejecting political correctness, about signaling political allegiance to a certain tribe that will not be lectured to by people who think they know better, and ultimately, about the right to believe that the virus was a hoax. For so long, truth had been presented to the pugnaciously unmasked as a matter of freedom rather than fact, and anyone who disagreed had a political agenda. And so, the fetishizing of freedom of speech meant that people were risking death to believe what they wanted to believe even when told otherwise, *especially* when they were told otherwise. Dying to "own" the libs.

This sort of fixating on the "other," the libs, immigrants, people of color, and their identity politics creates a friendly environment for the growing numbers of dangerous supremacist Identitarians. These white nationalist groups end up targeting everyone, not just minorities. They are murdering white citizens and plotting to kill white American Democratic politicians and white, high-profile left-wing figures.

"We willingly turned the other way on white supremacy because there were real political costs to talking about white supremacy," the national security strategist P. W. Singer said to the *New York Times* magazine in 2018. While we have been hyperventilating about cultural appropriation and "oppression Olympics," white supremacist groups have been gathering momentum away from the limelight. The Proud Boys, a white nationalist hate group that emerged as a powerful street force when it helped organize the coalition of the far-right groups' march in Charlottesville, was officially founded in late 2016. But its founder, Gavin McInnes, has been writing publicly and giving interviews, honing his violent misogynistic, Islamophobic, racist politics for at least a decade preceding that. Momentum for the group had been gathering for years before Trump's election gave them space to flourish. Violence is one of their four levels of membership described by McInnes as a privilege. "You get beat up, kick the crap out of an antifa," is how he described it in 2017. By the time they became, as *Vox* describes, "the shock troops of the weirdo right," the media had about a decade of catching up to do if it was going to accurately report the group's threat.

In the United States, the identity that has posed the most serious threat to internal security did not come from outside the country. A report by the Anti-Defamation League's Center on Extremism revealed that the overwhelming majority, 71 percent, of politically motivated extremist deaths in the US in the ten years preceding 2017 were at the hands of far-right or white-supremacist ideologues. The proportion of such crimes committed in the same timeframe by Islamic extremists, the focus of the country's counterterrorism strategy? Just 26 percent.

But the excepting of whiteness still runs so deep that these numbers have had little effect on the country's counterterrorism approach, which is still focused primarily on jihadists. Between 2002 and 2017, according to the Stimson Center, the United States spent $2.8 trillion on counterterrorism, which was channeled mainly toward investigating foreign- and US-born jihadis. In that period, attacks by Muslim extremists resulted in one hundred deaths. Between 2008 and 2017 alone, domestic extremists killed 387 people.

In that light, does it make sense that the first national security measure taken by the Trump administration was to ban visitors from Muslim countries? Not at all. It's dog whistling while Rome burns. The boomerang effect is evident in the profiles of the dead. They are Heather Heyer, mowed down at a far-right rally in Virginia in 2017. They are Taliesin Myrddin Namkai-Meche and Rick Best, two men stabbed to death on a train in 2017, when they intervened to prevent a racist attack. They are Garrett Foster, shot to death at a Black Lives Matter rally in 2020 in Texas.

Racial politics also backfire in other less obvious, but in aggregate life-shortening, ways. In *Dying of Whiteness: How the Politics of Racial Resentment Is Killing America's Heartland*, author Jonathan M. Metzl argues that the cultural associations of "whiteness" encourage white people to adopt political views, such as opposition to gun laws or the Affordable Care Act, that reduce their own life expectancy. "They could look at the wealthy persons or corporations or donors who were actually causing policies that were worsening their lives, or they could look at the people they believed were taking away their resources," Metzl summarized in a *Vox* interview. "And they chose, electorally, to look at the latter—and that's hurting nearly everybody."

Little demonstrates the hurt "nearly everybody" suffers when voters look only at people they think are taking away their resources than the calamitous coronavirus death toll in the United States. In supporting a president who promised them status over others, as opposed to one who would be competent as a commander in chief, Trump voters ensured that America did not stand a chance against the virus. The pandemic was indifferent to Trump's bluster. "Mugged by Reality," is how the *New York Times* described a flailing president who only knew how to leverage myths to get his way. He minimized the threat of the virus, then botched the response, delaying lockdowns and fighting with governors, then fished in his bag for the usual tricks—the virus was the fault of foreigners and Chinese people, lefties were trying to kill the economy, mask wearing was political correctness. As he continued this diversionary routine, instead of mobilizing resources for personal protective equipment for hospital staff or increasing the capacity for ventilators, the body count rose. The United States of America, the country with the highest GDP in the world, ended up with the largest coronavirus death toll in the world.

And on it goes—a civilization in decline comforting itself, diverting itself from its decay by resorting to myths of grandeur. There are very few real winners here, but the perception of winning deceives the losers into submission.

Myths are hierarchy stabilizers; they keep power structures standing, creating the illusion of status by concentrating on relative status. If attention can be maintained on how you are better off than someone below you, it can be diverted from the fact that there is someone above you who is either exploiting you or enjoying more unearned privileges than you. If attention can be maintained on how those below you are coming for your resources, then your eyes are fixed downward, never upward. By their very nature, hierarchies only have one small group at the top. Believing in a myth is sort of like taking part in a Ponzi scheme. You are constantly being told that your stake is accruing, sometimes you might even get a dividend, but ultimately only the scheme owners make any real money. There is no real value created, the scheme eventually collapses, and the money winners abscond with the spoils.

Legend has it that the moment it became clear that Donald Trump won, around three in the morning (EST), David Remnick of the *New Yorker* sat down and wrote his now famous piece, "An American Tragedy," in one sitting. It started with the assertion: "The election of Donald Trump to the Presidency is nothing less than a tragedy for the American republic, a tragedy for the Constitution, and a triumph for the forces, at home and abroad, of nativism, authoritarianism, misogyny, and racism." Remnick, in the small hours of that morning, came ever so close to the heart of it. He had no time for those who were waiting in the wings, rightly predicted, to normalize Trump, to stress the innate decency of the American people and minimize the darkness that elected him. But once Remnick is spent and his affection for his desecrated America rises again, he ends on a note of exceptionalism.

"But despair is no answer. To combat authoritarianism, to call out lies, to struggle honorably and fiercely in the name of American ideals—that is what is left to do."

It does not occur to Remnick, even as he warns against the complacencies of belief in an inherently virtuous America, that maybe the forces of nativism, authoritarianism, misogyny, and racism do, in fact, also embody America. Who is to say which set of these competing ideas is the definitive one? We must start earlier—the American Tragedy was happening all along.

None of the things that myths preach against, from defensive identity politics activism to the necessity of political correctness, would be necessary in a world where Remnick's cushion of "ideals" existed. But we are not there yet. The greatest trick a myth can play is to convince people that we are in the best of all possible worlds.

New Stories

In June 2020, I realized I had made a mistake. I had always been supportive of any demands for the removal of statues linked to slavery, but it was a lukewarm support. My backing was out of principle, rather than passionate conviction. My position was that if statues of slave traders made people uncomfortable, then it is their right that they are removed out of respect for those whose feelings are hurt. But I had no emotional connection to the matter. I hadn't grown up as a minority in a white country which had enslaved my ancestors. I was a black woman who grew up in a black country. I became racialized only once I moved to the United Kingdom.

And then on a balmy day in June 2020, Back Lives Matter protestors, spurred on by the murder of George Floyd, made their way to a square in Bristol, England, where the statue of Edward Colston, a seventeenth-century English merchant and slave trader, had stood for years. They tore down the statue, dragged it to the harbor, and heaved it into the very waters in which his slave ships docked.

I was overwhelmed with an emotion that came with no warning. I hadn't realized how much any gestures of respect, any concessions to basic demands, had been withheld from black people. I hadn't realized until that moment what had happened to me as a result of living in a country that will not even extend the most fundamental of dignities to black people. That will not acknowledge their history. That will not admit that its prosperity is built on the backs of colonialism and enslavement of people of color from the West Indies to the Indian subcontinent. I had been made small. I had been rendered invisible. I had been made to believe that things like tearing down statues were marginal issues, because I believed that I deserved less than the right to walk down the street and not have a slave trader stand glorified over me every day.

Colston had been the subject of many petitions for removal. The authorities mired the process in the treacle of bureaucracy. That bureaucracy itself was a result of the reluctance of authorities to engage with the country's history of slavery. And so, the protestors took matters into their own hands and dragged Colston into the river.

The emotion that stung my eyes that moment was also the stirring of hope and of faith in something I always knew at heart but had perhaps become jaded about. Change is always possible. Change isn't inevitable, but it is always possible.

The myths that subvert freedom work hard to prevent change from happening. They are powerful. But they are not all-powerful. They depend on killing anger and suffocating the fire of justice denied. They work by bamboozling you with all sorts of logic that makes you think maybe your complaint is unreasonable. Maybe things aren't that bad. Maybe there are other priorities. I had written a whole book about myths, and when Colston came down realized I myself had been fooled into thinking, you know, there are more important things than statues. I had been tricked by all the tools myths deploy to make you shrink and keep cutting more corners off your ambition. Statues are important. Incarceration rates are important. Everything is important when you are fighting for equality.

In moments like the ones that came after the Black Lives Matter protests, it becomes clear how much change can happen, and how quickly it can happen. It becomes clear how myths are in the end just stories that lose their hold when people simply refuse to believe them anymore. All those arguments in the US and the UK about how monuments and statues were in fact not about race, but about history, sheepishly receded when enough people no longer indulged them.

The global reaction to Black Lives Matter is still unfolding while I write these words. But so far, in the space of just a month, statues and monuments were removed in the United Kingdom, Belgium, and all over the United States. Four statues to Christopher Columbus were brought down, as well as those memorializing John C. Calhoun and Jefferson Davis. With the removal of every single one I felt the same stirring of hope, the same resurgence of an anger nourished and multiplied by my suppression of it.

In the same month, the Mississippi legislature passed a bill to change the state flag to one that does not include the Confederate battle flag. NASCAR banned the Confederate flag altogether. The chief of naval operations tweeted that he had "directed [my] staff to begin crafting an order that would prohibit the Confederate battle flag from all public spaces and work areas aboard Navy installations, ships, aircraft and submarines." New York repealed 50-a, the law that mandates keeping police personnel records secret. It was a law that activists had been campaigning to overturn for years. The June protests gave their efforts the edge needed for the repeal. In continental Europe, after two weeks of Black Lives Matter–associated protests against police brutality toward France's minority populations, France imposed a ban on police using chokeholds when arresting suspects.

In the media world, subterranean fissures that had been growing for years cracked the surface. The *New York Times* ran an op-ed by Senator Tom Cotton that called for sending in the troops to suppress the Black Lives Matter protests and "restore order." Several *Times* journalists who had for years grumbled quietly about the maximalist free speech attitude of the paper's opinion pages, revolted. They began to post on social media that the op-ed put their black colleagues' lives at risk. Up to this point, senior editors at the paper stuck stubbornly to the defense that the op-ed pages are not the place to impose any value judgments or any fact-checking standards. This excuse, in the light of the clear threat to black lives, no longer held. Cotton's op-ed was not taken down, but a note was appended to it. The message said:

> *After publication, this essay met strong criticism from many readers (and many Times colleagues), prompting editors to review the piece and the editing process. Based on that review, we have concluded that the essay fell short of our standards and should not have been published.*
>
> *The basic arguments advanced by Senator Cotton—however objectionable people may find them—represent a newsworthy part of the current debate. But given the life-and-death importance of the topic, the senator's influential position and the gravity of the steps he advocates, the essay should have undergone the highest level of scrutiny.*

The paper finally got it. "Given the life-and-death importance of the topic," free speech could not be absolute. The op-ed editor resigned, and the paper continued to have important and fruitful internal discussions about its responsibility toward minorities under threat.

This process of self-reflection and making amends has forced media institutions to initiate changes that their black and ethnic minority staff have been demanding for years. Stan Wischnowski, editor of the *Philadelphia Inquirer*, resigned after the publication of a piece criticizing Black Lives Matter called "Buildings Matter Too." Journalists of color at the paper wrote an open letter to management declaring that they were "tired of shouldering the burden of dragging this two-hundred-year-old institution kicking and screaming into a more equitable age. We're tired of being told of the progress the company has made, and of being served platitudes about 'diversity and inclusion' when we raise our concerns."

Platitudes were no longer enough. Meetings with staff and resignations were followed up with concrete measures. In mid-June, the *Washington Post* announced more than a dozen new jobs focusing on race. In August, the paper appointed a managing editor for diversity and inclusion. Similar efforts are underway at other media institutions and publishing houses both in the United States and Europe. All of these measures had been demanded before. None of them was close to being achieved when George Floyd walked into a bodega to buy some cigarettes. The summer of 2020 changed the world.

This change was only possible because enough people came together to enforce their own lived reality, rejecting the myth that identity politics is a destructive force. This change was only possible because enough people finally recognized that all the argumentative tools that chilled their anger were merely devices, roadblocks on the path to freedom, rather than legitimate excuses. This kind of change will continue to be possible only if enough people make it their business to combat all the convincing and powerful myths that are constantly renewed to shame and dispirit us into submission.

No sooner had Black Lives Matter made some headway than the public discourse pivoted to the alleged crisis of "cancel culture." A letter published by *Harper's* magazine in July 2020, and signed by a prestigious group of writers, academics, and thinkers, stated that "our cultural institutions are facing a moment of trial. Powerful protests for racial and social justice are leading to overdue demands for police reform, along with wider calls for greater equality and inclusion across our society, not least in higher education, journalism, philanthropy, and the arts. But this needed reckoning has also intensified a new set of moral attitudes and political commitments that tend to weaken our norms of open debate and toleration of differences in favor of ideological conformity."

Airwaves and column inches that had until the publication of the letter been full of the promise and swagger of the Black Lives Matter gains became filled with invective and bickering about cancel culture. Was cancel culture real? Did the success of the 2020 Black Lives Matter movement now pose a threat by imposing a new orthodoxy of imagined race grievance? Is Twitter "editing the *New York Times*"? Before we could even count our few blessings, a new myth, that of cancel culture, attempted to rip those blessings out of our hands. The function of myths, to subvert freedom, is so finely tuned that in the summer of 2020 it almost felt automated. The myth machine had sensed that there was disturbance to the status quo, and it mobilized, spitting out cancel culture to divert us from the cause of racial equality.

Some members of our intellectual elite are so steeped in the fear of change, so wired by toxic myths that make them suspicious of revolutionary movements that *they* do not lead or have a role in, that they took one look at the largest global movement for equality in a generation, and the only thing they saw was a threat to "open debate." They looked at a world where, rightly, hitherto immune editors finally faced the consequences for irresponsible exercise of free speech that put others' lives at risk, and the only thing they saw was a threat to the jobs of an anointed class of narrators. They looked at a world where, for the first time, a large number of people who had no way of reaching that anointed class of narrators finally gained the

digital means to feed their opinions back, and all they saw was a bay-
ing mob. So effectively had grass roots movements, students, youth,
and identity activism been smeared over the years that instead of
welcoming change, our narrators fear it. The language of mythology,
and its concepts and classifications have become so widely distributed, so deeply entrenched in our popular culture and discourse,
that instead of freedom fighters, we see vandals. Instead of moral
courage, we see virtue signaling. Instead of kindness and sensitivity
to others, we see safetyism. Instead of accountability, we see cancel culture.

The good news is that one of the reasons these myths are strong
and getting stronger is that the causes they are fighting are also getting stronger. There are more of us fighting for freedom and equality.
And there are more of us in places where we have previously not been
allowed. There are more women, more people of color, more LGBTQ+
people in public life, and more allies turning up for us. We are writing books, we are being elected, we are filling newsrooms and boardrooms and swelling the streets of our cities with protest and demand
and a sense of ownership and entitlement that cannot be undone. We
are a threat to those who have always had an advantage over us.

But it's not enough that you and I exist, it's important that we
also light the little fires that we can. It's important that we also stake
our claim to our stories.

You see, the strength of myths is not in facts, but in the narrative. It is in the actual stories. The "facts" myths use are just conduits, devices that transport and plant the myths, like the fronds
of a flying dandelion seed. And so, it is pointless to fight fake facts,
or true but cynically twisted facts, with other facts. The new stories
we need to tell are not just the corrections of old stories, they are

visions, certainty that we have a choice, belief in the fact that for societies to evolve an old order must change. We cannot pick and choose the elements of progress that suit our own demographic or preferences because that eventually breaks down the whole machine. We have to be unapologetic about the reality that for civilizations to advance, their societies and political processes must be updated and refreshed. Ways of life that do not modify themselves to live up to their ideals will inevitably disintegrate. The only way to preserve the good that exists in our societies today is to allow it to wreck the bad.

So let them mock our wokeness, our safe spaces, our trigger warnings, our virtue signaling, and our cancel culture. Be strong in the knowledge that all these smears come from a place of fear. Rest assured that you are the latest in a long line of people who over the years have asked and been denied, but never gave up until they secured the rights you enjoy today. Seek comfort in your allies in a movement for equality that is strong and large and gentle with its members and resolute. Be confident in the belief that our fight is necessary, that our goals are noble. Remind yourself, when the counterinsurgency gets in your head, that what you seek is not retribution, but justice, equality, freedom, and peace for all.

We will get there. It will not be easy, and it will not happen overnight. But one thing is certain as far as the keepers of the status quo are concerned: it is already too late. They will be hearing from us.

Notes

10 **"found a number of instances of coverage"**: "From the Editors; The *Times* and Iraq," *New York Times*, May 26, 2004, accessed July 25, 2019, https://www.nytimes.com/2004/05/26/world/from-the-editors-the-times-and-iraq.html.

11 **"did not pay enough attention to voices"**: Gary Younge, "*Washington Post* Apologises for Underplaying WMD Scepticism," *Guardian*, August 13, 2004, accessed July 25, 2019, https://www.theguardian.com/world/2004/aug/13/pressandpublishing.usa.

11 **"We feel regret—but no shame"**: The Editors, "Were We Wrong?" *New Republic*, June 28, 2004, accessed July 25, 2019, https://newrepublic.com/article/67651/were-we-wrong.

11 **"It is now obvious"**: Thomas Friedman, "Time for Plan B," *New York Times*, August 4, 2006, accessed July 25, 2019, https://www.nytimes.com/2006/08/04/opinion/04friedman.html.

12 **"Off the Island"**: Thomas Friedman, "Vote France Off the Island," *New York Times*, February 9, 2003, accessed July 25, 2019, https://www.nytimes.com/2003/02/09/opinion/vote-france-off-the-island.html.

12 **"I was wrong on Iraq"**: Fareed Zakaria (@FareedZakaria), "I was wrong on Iraq," Twitter, October 26, 2015, 12:23 p.m., https://twitter.com/fareedzakaria/status/658725616720715776?lang=en; Fareed Zakaria, "Iraq War Was a Terrible Mistake," CNN, October 26, 2015, accessed July 25, 2019, https://edition.cnn.com/2015/10/26/opinions/zakaria-iraq-war-lessons/index.html.

12 **"Ten years after the war began"**: David Aaronovitch, "Now We Know Why

It Was Right to Invade Iraq," *Times* (London), February 21, 2013, accessed July 25, 2019, https://www.thetimes.co.uk/article/now-we-know-why-it-was-right-to-invade-iraq-b9tsvq7l2xz.

12	**"Ten years on, the case for invading Iraq is still valid":** Nick Cohen, "Ten Years On, the Case for Invading Iraq Is Still Valid," *Observer*, March 3, 2013, accessed July 25, 2019, https://www.theguardian.com/commentisfree/2013/mar/03/10-years-right-invaded-iraq.

13	**"Arab Spring" from "the top down":** Thomas Friedman, "Saudi Arabia's Arab Spring, at Last," *New York Times*, November 23, 2017, accessed July 25, 2019, https://www.nytimes.com/2017/11/23/opinion/saudi-prince-mbs-arab-spring.html.

14	**"one of the most exclusive middle-class professions":** Patrick Wintour, "Student Fees for Those Who Live at Home Should Be Axed—Report," *Guardian*, July 19, 2009, accessed July 25, 2019, https://www.theguardian.com/politics/2009/jul/19/fees-home-students-axed.

15	**Research in 2016 by the American Society of News Editors:** "Table 0—Employees by Minority Group" (originally published by the ASNE, now the NLA, 2019), accessed July 25, 2019, https://members.newsleaders.org/content.asp?contentid=147.

15	**"a typical white, male-centric newsroom":** Tal Abbady, "The Modern Newsroom Is Stuck Behind the Gender and Color Line," *Code Switch*, NPR, May 1, 2017, accessed July 25, 2019, https://www.npr.org/sections/codeswitch/2017/05/01/492982066/the-modern-newsroom-is-stuck-behind-the-gender-and-color-line.

18	**US newsroom employees are more likely to be white:** Elizabeth Grieco, "Newsroom Employees Are Less Diverse Than US Workers Overall" (Pew Research Center, November 2, 2018), accessed October 30, 2020, https://www.pewresearch.org/fact-tank/2018/11/02/newsroom-employees-are-less-diverse-than-u-s-workers-overall/.

CHAPTER TWO

20	**"Privacy rights threatened":** Carlos Maza, "Fox Nation Touts Fake Story About Transgender Student Harassing Girls in School Bathroom" (Media Matters for America, October 15, 2013), accessed October 30, 2020, https://www.mediamatters.org/fox-nation/fox-nation-touts-fake-story-about-transgender-student-harassing-girls-school-bathroom.

21 **entire account was based on the complaint of a single parent:** Sunnivie Bry-
dum, "Mother of Trans Teen Targeted by Right-Wingers Speaks Out," *Advocate*, October 21, 2013, accessed October 30, 2020, https://www.advocate.com
/politics/transgender/2013/10/21/mother-trans-teen-targeted-right-wingers
-speaks-out; Carlos Maza, "Fox Nation Touts Fake Story About Transgender
Student Harassing Girls in School Bathroom," Media Matters for America,
October 15, 2013, accessed January 4, 2021, https://www.mediamatters.org/
fox-nation/fox-nation-touts-fake-story-about-transgender-student-harassing
-girls-school-bathroom.

21 **This change suggests a realization:** "Nightmare: Teen Boy Harasses
Girls in Their Bathroom, Colo. School Tells Girls They Have No Rights,"
Pacific Justice Institute, October 10, 2013, accessed January 4, 2021, https://
www.pacificjustice.org/press/nightmare-teen-boy-harasses-girls-in-their
-bathroom-colo-school-tells-girls-they-have-no-rights/; "Update: Colo.
School District Weighs New Trangender Proposal," Pacific Justice Institute,
January 15, 2014, accessed January 4, 2021, https://www.pacificjustice.org
/press/update-colo-school-district-weighs-new-transgender-proposal/.

22 **According to 2018 research by the nonprofit More in Common:** Stephen
Hawkins, Daniel Yudkin, Míriam Juan-Torres, and Tim Dixon, *Hidden
Tribes: A Study of America's Polarized Landscape* (New York: More in Common, 2018), accessed October 30, 2020, https://hiddentribes.us/pdf/hidden_
tribes_report.pdf.

22 **perception that politically correct norms have taken hold:** Lucian Gideon
Conway III, "How a Cultural Revolt Against 'Political Correctness' Helped
Launch Trump into the Presidency," LSE US Centre, February 28, 2018,
accessed October 30, 2020, https://blogs.lse.ac.uk/usappblog/2018/02/28/
how-a-cultural-revolt-against-political-correctness-helped-launch-trump
-into-the-presidency/.

22 **According to Nick Adams:** Adam Geller and Bryna Godar, "'No More Political Correctness' for Trump Supporters," Associated Press, April 10, 2016,
accessed October 30, 2020, https://www.pbs.org/newshour/politics/no-more
-political-correctness-for-trump-supporters.

23 **Suicide rates for transgender:** Gwen Aviles, "Comedian's Death Under-
scores High Suicide Rate Among Transgender People," NBC News, October
10, 2019, accessed October 30, 2020, https://www.nbcnews.com/feature/nbc
-out/comedian-s-death-underscores-high-suicide-rate-among-transgender
-people-n1067546.

23 **Black transgender women:** *A National Epidemic: Fatal Anti-Transgender Violence in the United States in 2019* (Washington, DC: Human Rights Campaign Foundation, 2019), accessed October 30, 2020, https://assets2.hrc.org/files/assets/resources/Anti-TransViolenceReport2019.pdf?_ga=2.159347002.1054893377.1604062911-108311927.1604062911.

23 **FBI revealed that attacks:** Adeel Hassan, "Hate-Crime Violence Hits 16-Year High, FBI Reports," *New York Times*, November 12, 2019, accessed October 30, 2020, https://www.nytimes.com/2019/11/12/us/hate-crimes-fbi-report.html.

25 **"falling over themselves in their rush":** Roger Kimball, *Tenured Radicals: How Politics Has Corrupted Our Higher Education* (New York: Harper and Row, 1990), quoted in Jonathan Yardley, "Radical Revolution on Campus," *Washington Post*, June 6, 1990, accessed July 23, 2019, https://www.washingtonpost.com/archive/lifestyle/1990/06/06/radical-revolution-on-campus/66ec7e09-721f-4397-95f1-cdbcd1ffb6e8/?utm_term=.fbfd71691bbf.

27 **"appearance of a critical mass of people":** Nancy Baker Jones, "Confronting the PC 'Debate': The Politics of Identity and the American Image," *NWSA Journal* 6, no. 3 (Autumn 1994): 386, accessed October 30, 2020, https://www.jstor.org/stable/4316352?seq=1#metadata_info_tab_contents

28 **"the queers" of the '90s:** Robert Weissberg, quoted in John K. Wilson, *The Myth of Political Correctness: The Conservative Attack on Higher Education* (Durham, NC: Duke University Press, 1995), 16.

30 **unrestrained hiring and employment practices:** "Through Foam," *Harvard Crimson*, October 22, 1985, accessed October 30, 2020, https://www.thecrimson.com/article/1985/10/22/through-foam-pbcboors-beer-has-kicked/; James Coates, "Will Coors Swallow the Union Label?" *Chicago Tribune*, December 11, 1988, accessed January 5, 2021, https://www.chicagotribune.com/news/ct-xpm-1988-12-11-8802230657-story.html#:~:text=It%20was%20disclosed%20by%20the,users%2C%20and%20other%20personal%20matters; B. Erin Cole and Allyson Brantley, "The Coors Boycott: When a Beer Can Signaled Your Politics," CPR News (Colorado Public Radio), October 3, 2014, accessed January 5, 2021, https://www.cpr.org/2014/10/03/the-coors-boycott-when-a-beer-can-signaled-your-politics/; Beverly Morris, "Case Study: Coors Beer and AFL-CIO Slug It Out in the Media" (case study, New Jersey Institute of Technology, October 2011), accessed January 5, 2021, https://web.njit.edu/~bmorris/case_study.pdf.

31 **foundation's stated mission:** "About Heritage," Heritage Foundation, https://www.heritage.org/about-heritage/mission.

32 **"longtime libertarians":** Jane Mayer, "Covert Operations: The Billionaire Brothers Who Are Waging a War Against Obama," *New Yorker*, August 30, 2010, accessed July 23, 2019, https://www.newyorker.com/magazine/2010/08/30/covert-operations.

33 **"wrongs don't make a right":** Harvey C. Mansfield Jr., "Political Correctness and the Suicide of the Intellect" (lecture, Heritage Foundation colloquium, Washington, DC, June 26, 1991), https://www.heritage.org/node/10058/print-display.

33 **"We mustn't let things get by that we know are wrong":** Mansfield, "Political Correctness."

35 **"did not arise from grassroots movements":** Wilson, *The Myth of Political Correctness*, 25.

35 **"no sooner was it invoked as a genuine standard for sociopolitical practice":** Ruth Perry, "Historically Correct," *Women's Review of Books* 9, no. 5 (February 1992): 16.

36 **"political correctness has ignited controversy across the land":** Kat Chow, " 'Politically Correct': The Phrase Has Gone from Wisdom to Weapon," *Code Switch*, NPR, December 14, 2016, accessed July 23, 2019, https://www.npr.org/sections/codeswitch/2016/12/14/505324427/politically-correct-the-phrase-has-gone-from-wisdom-to-weapon?t=1562162061694.

37 **"Political correctness . . . is a catch-all term":** Amanda Taub, "The Truth About 'Political Correctness' Is That It Doesn't Actually Exist," *Vox*, January 28, 2015, accessed October 30, 2020, https://www.vox.com/2015/1/28/7930845/political-correctness-doesnt-exist.

38 **"evidence suggests that Trump's grandiose rhetorical style":** Lucian Gideon Conway III, Meredith A. Repke, and Shannon C. Houck, "Donald Trump as a Cultural Revolt Against Perceived Communication Restriction: Priming Political Correctness Norms Causes More Trump Support," *Journal of Social and Political Psychology* 5, no. 1, (2017): 246.

39 **"norms of restrictive communication":** Conway et al., "Donald Trump as a Cultural Revolt.

40 **"Having elevated the powers of PC to mythic status":** Moira Weigel, "Political Correctness: How the Right Invented a Phantom Enemy," *Guardian*, November 30, 2016, accessed July 23, 2019, https://www.theguardian.com/

us-news/2016/nov/30/political-correctness-how-the-right-invented-phantom-enemy-donald-trump.

42 **Trump decided that the WHO:** The White House, "President Donald J. Trump Is Demanding Accountability from the World Health Organization," April 15, 2020, accessed October 30, 2020, https://www.whitehouse.gov/briefings-statements/president-donald-j-trump-demanding-accountability-world-health-organization/.

43 **"They've landed on attacking the left":** Rebecca Traister, "How Far-Right Media Is Weaponizing Coronavirus," *Cut*, March 24, 2020, accessed October 30, 2020, https://www.thecut.com/2020/03/how-far-right-media-is-weaponizing-coronavirus.html.

43 **did not lead to a spike in infections:** Dhaval M. Dave et al., "Black Lives Matter Protests, Social Distancing, and COVID-19" (Working Paper 27408, NBER Working Paper Series, National Bureau of Economic Research, Cambridge, MA, June 2020), accessed October 30, 2020, https://www.nber.org/system/files/working_papers/w27408/w27408.pdf.

43 **"low infection rates reflect":** Chelsea Janes, "Protests Probably Didn't Lead to Coronavirus Spikes, but It's Hard to Know for Sure," *Washington Post*, July 1, 2020, accessed October 30, 2020, https://www.washingtonpost.com/health/protests-probably-didnt-lead-to-coronavirus-spikes-but-its-hard-to-know-for-sure/2020/06/30/d8179678-baf5-11ea-8cf5-9c1b8d7f84c6_story.html.

44 **"I understand where he's coming from":** Matt Perez, "Trump on Advisor Comparing Lockdown Protesters to Rosa Parks: 'Strong Statement,'" *Forbes*, April 18, 2020, accessed October 30, 2020, https://www.forbes.com/sites/mattperez/2020/04/18/trump-on-adviser-comparing-lockdown-protesters-to-rosa-parks-strong-statement/?sh=75a9d980521f.

45 **"While the Muslim community has the right":** Edward Wyatt, "3 Republicans Criticize Obama's Endorsement of Mosque," *New York Times*, August 14, 2010, accessed October 30, 2020, https://www.nytimes.com/2010/08/15/us/politics/15reaction.html.

45 **built near Ground Zero:** Donald Trump (@realdonaldtrump), "Ground Zero Mosque should not go up where planned. It is wrong. My offer still stands to buy the property. Good deal for everyone," Twitter, December 10, 2012, 5:45 p.m., https://twitter.com/realdonaldtrump/status/278269256657956865?lang=en.

47 **"I believe that everybody has a right to be in the United States":** Adam Serwer, "The Nationalist's Delusion," *Atlantic*, November 20, 2017, accessed July

25, 2019, https://www.theatlantic.com/politics/archive/2017/11/the-national
ists-delusion/546356/.

49 **"controversy over *The Bell Curve*"**: Ezra Klein, "Sam Harris, Charles Murray, and the Allure of Race Science," *Vox*, March 27, 2018, accessed July 25,
2019,   https://www.vox.com/policy-and-politics/2018/3/27/15695060/sam
-harris-charles-murray-race-iq-forbidden-knowledge-podcast-bell-curve.

49 **"This isn't 'forbidden knowledge'"**: Klein, "Sam Harris, Charles Murray,
and the Allure of Race Science."

50 **feted in the *New York Times***: Bari Weiss, "Meet the Renegades of the Intellectual Dark Web," *New York Times*, May 8, 2018, accessed July 25, 2019, https://
www.nytimes.com/2018/05/08/opinion/intellectual-dark-web.html.

51 **"lit the flame"**: Patrick Wintour, "Hillary Clinton: Europe Must Curb Immigration to Stop Rightwing Populists," *Guardian*, November 22, 2018, accessed
July 25, 2019, https://www.theguardian.com/world/2018/nov/22/hillary
-clinton-europe-must-curb-immigration-stop-populists-trump-brexit.

51 **"populist correctness"**: Arwa Mahdawi, "Populist Correctness: The New PC
Culture of Trump's America and Brexit Britain," *Guardian*, February 19, 2017,
accessed July 25, 2019, https://www.theguardian.com/commentisfree/2017
/feb/19/populist-correctness-new-pc-culture-trump-america-brexit-britain.

51 **"Offends"**: "Offends," Kemp for Governor campaign ad, July 16, 2018,
accessed July 25, 2019, YouTube video, https://www.youtube.com/watch?v=
-3irfSQZZyw.

52 **caught on tape complaining**: David Gilbert, "Trump Secures Georgia Win
for Brian Kemp, Who Wants to 'Round Up' Illegals in His Pickup Truck,"
Vice, July 25, 2018, https://news.vice.com/en_us/article/a3qkv8/trump-georgia
-brian-kemp-governor.

52 **"if Kemp wins his runoff"**: Ed Kilgore, " 'Political Incorrectness' Is Just
'Political Correctness' for Conservatives," *New York*, July 17, 2018, accessed
July 25, 2019, http://nymag.com/intelligencer/2018/07/anti-pc-is-political
-correctness-for-the-right.html.

52 **"coded cover"**: Polly Toynbee, "This Bold Equality Push Is Just What We
Needed. In 1997," *Guardian*, April 28, 2009, accessed July 25, 2019, https://
www.theguardian.com/commentisfree/2009/apr/28/toynbee-equality-bill
-welfare.

53 **"matter of replacing one set of authorities and dogmas"**: Edward W. Said,
Reflections on Exile and Other Essays (Cambridge, MA: Harvard University
Press, 2001), 381.

CHAPTER THREE

57 **"wide cross section" of Americans:** Maeve Duggan, "Online Harassment 2017," Pew Research Center, July 11, 2017, accessed July 25, 2019, https://www.pewinternet.org/2017/07/11/online-harassment-2017/.

58 **"97 percent of domestic violence programs":** "Recognizing and Combating Technology-Facilitated Abuse," National Network to End Domestic Violence, October 13, 2016, accessed October 30, 2020, https://nnedv.org/latest_update/combating-technology-facilitated-abuse/.

58 **Women's Aid reported:** "Women's Experiences of Violence and Abuse on Twitter," *Toxic Twitter* (London: Amnesty International, March 2018), accessed October 30, 2020, https://www.amnesty.org/en/latest/research/2018/03/online-violence-against-women-chapter-3/.

61 **"has never accepted an absolutist interpretation":** Christopher Wolfe, "The Limits of Free Speech (Book Review)," *Review of Politics* 48, no. 1 (Winter 1986): 139, accessed July 25, 2019, https://search.proquest.com/openview/9d9d438f2304ff12be298b07179f651e/1?pq-origsite=gschol-ar&cbl=1820944.

63 **"suppression of noxious ideas does not defeat them":** Danuta Kean, "Free-Speech Groups Defend Publication of Milo Yiannopoulos Memoir," *Guardian*, January 6, 2017, accessed July 25, 2019, https://www.theguardian.com/books/2017/jan/06/free-speech-groups-defend-publication-of-milo-yiannoploulos-memoir.

64 **"When his comments about pedophilia/pederasty came to light":** Roxane Gay, "All I really need to say," Tumblr post, February 20, 2017, accessed July 25, 2019, http://web.archive.org/web/20200312225007/https://roxanegay.tumblr.com/post/157506508260/all-i-really-need-to-say.

66 **"there's a fundamental mission that we're serving":** Jason Koebler and Joseph Cox, "How Twitter Sees Itself," *Vice*, October 7, 2019, accessed October 30, 2020, https://www.vice.com/en/article/a35nbj/twitter-content-moderation.

66 **almost eleven million accounts were reported:** Danielle Abril, "Twitter's User-Reported Violations Jumped 19%—but the Number of Accounts Punished Dropped," *Fortune*, May 10, 2019, accessed October 30, 2020, https://fortune.com/2019/05/10/twitter-transparency-report-abuse/.

67 **Twitter was spending:** Open Secrets, s.v. "Client Profile: Twitter," last updated October 23, 2020, accessed October 30, 2020, https://www.opensecrets.org/federal-lobbying/clients/summary?cycle=2018&id=D000067113.

67 **In the same year, Facebook's lobbying:** Open Secrets, s.v. "Client Profile: Facebook Inc," last updated October 23, 2020, accessed October 30, 2020, https://www.opensecrets.org/federal-lobbying/clients/summary?cycle=2019&id=D000033563.

68 **Appearing on BBC's *Newsnight*:** "What Do Far-Right Extremism and Islamist Extremism Have in Common?" *Newsnight*, BBC, June 19, 2017, accessed July 25, 2019, https://www.youtube.com/watch?v=XGNEZr11LFE.

69 **"privileging of freedom of speech over freedom to life":** Liz Fekete, letter to the editor, *Guardian,* March 25, 2018, accessed July 25, 2019, https://www.theguardian.com/world/2018/mar/25/freedom-of-speech-or-freedom-to-life.

73 **"These THUGS are dishonoring the memory":** Donald Trump (@realdonaldtrump), "....These THUGS are dishonoring the memory of George Floyd, and I won't let that happen. Just spoke to Governor Tim Walz and told him that the Military is with him all the way. Any difficulty and we will assume control but, when the looting starts, the shooting starts. Thank you!" Twitter, May 29, 2020, 12:53 a.m., accessed October 30, 2020, https://twitter.com/realdonaldtrump/status/1266231100780744704.

74 **He accused Twitter of "interfering":** Sonam Sheth, "Trump Accuses Twitter of 'Interfering in the 2020 Presidential Election' after It Fact-Checked His False Tweets about Voting by Mail," *Business Insider*, May 27, 2020, accessed October 30, 2020, https://www.businessinsider.com/trump-accuses-twitter-interfering-2020-race-voting-ballot-fact-check-2020-5?IR=T.

74 **Trump warned (on Twitter):** Jon Sharman, "Trump Threatens to Close Down Social Media Platforms Which 'Silence Conservative Voices,' After Twitter Posts Warning under His Tweet," *Independent*, May 27, 2020, accessed October 30, 2020, https://www.independent.co.uk/news/world/americas/us-politics/trump-twitter-close-accounts-social-media-misinformation-policy-tweet-a9534681.html.

75 **On these grounds, a lawsuit was filed:** Alison Frankel and Nandita Bose, "Tech Advocacy Group's Lawsuit Says Trump's Order on Social Media Is Unconstitutional," Reuters, June 2, 2020, accessed October 30, 2020, https://www.reuters.com/article/us-twitter-trump-lawsuit-idUSKBN2392V9.

77 **"Free Speech Grifters":** Mari Uyehara, "The Free Speech Grifters," *GQ*, March 19, 2018, accessed July 25, 2019, https://www.gq.com/story/free-speech-grifting.

77 **"the motherlode of bad ideas":** Dan Cohen, "Bill Maher's Outrageous State-

ments about Islam and Muslims Are Beyond the Pale," *Salon*, February 23, 2017, accessed January 26, 2021, https://www.salon.com/2017/02/23/bill-maher-bigtime-bigot-his-outrageous-statements-about-islam-and-muslims-are-beyond-the-pale_partner/.

77 **"if Muslim men could get laid more"**: Nesrine Malik, "I Am Not Your Muslim," *Code Switch*, NPR, May 6, 2017, accessed January 26, 2021, https://www.npr.org/sections/codeswitch/2017/05/06/485548424/i-am-not-your-muslim.

77 **"Given the myopic focus on liberals"**: Uyehara, "The Free Speech Grifters."

78 **Research by Georgetown University's Free Speech Project:** Zack Beauchamp, "Data Shows a Surprising Campus Free Speech Problem: Left-Wingers Being Fired for Their Opinions," *Vox*, August 3, 2018, accessed February 17, 2021, https://www.vox.com/policy-and-politics/2018/8/3/17644180/political-correctness-free-speech-liberal-data-georgetown.

78 **overall public support for free speech has in fact risen over time:** Matthew Yglesias, "Everything We Think About the Political Correctness Debate Is Wrong," *Vox*, March 12, 2018, accessed July 25, 2019, https://www.vox.com/policy-and-politics/2018/3/12/17100496/political-correctness-data.

79 **"There is no campus free speech crisis"**: Jeffrey Adam Sachs, "There Is No Campus Free Speech Crisis: A Close Look at the Evidence," Niskanen Center, April 27, 2018, accessed October 30, 2020, https://niskanencenter.org/blog/there-is-no-campus-free-speech-crisis-a-close-look-at-the-evidence/.

80 **The report pointed out that the foundation's invitees:** Stephanie Saul, "The Conservative Force Behind Speeches Roiling College Campuses," *New York Times*, May 20, 2017, accessed October 30, 2020, https://www.nytimes.com/2017/05/20/us/college-conservative-speeches.html.

81 **NORC's General Social Survey research created:** NORC at the University of Chicago, "Tolerance Grows for a Wide Variety of Groups, Except for Muslim Extremists," press release, August 25, 2011, accessed October 30, 2020, https://www.norc.org/NewsEventsPublications/PressReleases/Pages/tolerance-grows-for-a-wide-variety-of-groups,-except-for-Muslim-extremists.aspx.

81 **Vox also found that the perception of Muslims:** Max Fisher and Amanda Taub, "*Vox* Got No Threats for Posting Charlie Hebdo Cartoons, Dozens for Covering Islamophobia," *Vox*, January 14, 2015, accessed October 30, 2020, https://www.vox.com/2015/1/14/7541095/charlie-hebdo-muslims-threats.

81 **"speaker disinvitation attempts have a higher success rate"**: Sean Stevens, "Campus Speaker Disinvitation Trends (Part 2 of 2)," Heterodox Academy,

February 7, 2017, accessed July 25, 2019, https://heterodoxacademy.org/blog
/campus-speaker-disinvitations-recent-trends-part-2-of-2/.

83 **"Today this speech restriction, tomorrow the Inquisition":** Magdalena
Jozwiak, "Internet, Freedom of Speech and Slippery Slope Argument—The
Case of the 'Right to Be Forgotten,'" (working paper, SSRN, March 15, 2018),
accessed July 25, 2019, http://dx.doi.org/10.2139/ssrn.3141370.

83 **"slippery slope arguments are however slippery themselves":** Jozwiak,
"Internet, Freedom of Speech and Slippery Slope Argument."

86 **"If free speech does take precedence":** Andrew Marantz, "How Social-
Media Trolls Turned UC Berkeley into a Free-Speech Circus," *New
Yorker*, June 25, 2018, accessed July 25, 2019, https://www.newyorker.com
/magazine/2018/07/02/how-social-media-trolls-turned-uc-berkeley-into-a
-free-speech-circus.

CHAPTER FOUR

88 **During his years of service:** "Officer Who Pressed Knee on George Floyd's
Neck Had Nearly 20 Complaints Against Him, Two Letters of Reprimand," Associated Press, May 28, 2020, accessed October 30, 2020, https://
www.theglobeandmail.com/world/article-officer-who-pressed-knee-on
-george-floyds-neck-had-nearly-2/.

91 **"actively committed to struggling":** Combahee River Collective, "A Black
Feminist Statement," April 1977, BlackPast.org, https://www.blackpast.org/
african-american-history/combahee-river-collective-statement-1977/.

91 **"We realize that the only people who care enough":** Combahee River Collective, "A Black Feminist Statement."

92 **"If Black women were free":** Combahee River Collective, "A Black Feminist
Statement."

93 **"We know that this is false":** Asad Haider, "Mistaken Identity: Race and
Class in the Age of Trump" (lecture, Elliott Bay Book Company, Seat-
tle, WA, May 3, 2018), accessed July 25, 2019, https://www.youtube.com
/watch?v=6vaZGh5CIPY.

94 **"politics of recognition":** Amy Chua, "How America's Identity Politics Went
from Inclusion to Division," *Guardian*, March 1, 2018, accessed July 25, 2019.
https://www.theguardian.com/society/2018/mar/01/how-americas-identity
-politics-went-from-inclusion-to-division.

94 **"fundamental belief that drove my dad":** "How a Rising Star of White

Nationalism Broke Free from the Movement," *Fresh Air*, NPR, September 24, 2018, accessed July 25, 2019, https://www.npr.org/2018/09/24/651052970/how-a-rising-star-of-white-nationalism-broke-free-from-the-movement.

95 **Lilla manages to blame the Trump "whitelash" on liberals:** Mark Lilla, "The End of Identity Liberalism," *New York Times*, November 18, 2016, accessed July 25, 2019, https://www.nytimes.com/2016/11/20/opinion/sunday/the-end-of-identity-liberalism.html.

96 **"I kind of feel that people are looking down on us":** Declan Walsh, "Alienated and Angry, Coal Miners See Donald Trump as Their Only Choice," *New York Times*, August 19, 2016, accessed July 25, 2019, https://www.nytimes.com/2016/08/20/world/americas/alienated-and-angry-coal-miners-see-donald-trump-as-their-only-choice.html.

97 **"Contrary to what some have suggested":** Matthew Fowler, Vladimir E. Medenica, and Cathy J. Cohen, "Why 41 Percent of White Millennials Voted for Trump," *Washington Post*, December 15, 2017, accessed July 25, 2019. https://www.washingtonpost.com/news/monkey-cage/wp/2017/12/15/racial-resentment-is-why-41-percent-of-white-millennials-voted-for-trump-in-2016/?utm_term=.9e49ac22dd79.

98 **perceptions of the American economy were influenced:** Michael Tesler, *Post-Racial or Most Racial? Race and Politics in the Obama Era* (Chicago: University of Chicago Press, 2016).

98 **"evidence is pretty clear":** Michael Tesler, "Economic Anxiety Isn't Driving Racial Resentment. Racial Resentment Is Driving Economic Anxiety," *Washington Post*, August 22, 2016, accessed July 25, 2019, https://www.washingtonpost.com/news/monkey-cage/wp/2016/08/22/economic-anxiety-isnt-driving-racial-resentment-racial-resentment-is-driving-economic-anxiety/?utm_term=.1ab-d02035e0e.

99 **"it used to be a pretty good deal":** Niraj Chokshi, "Trump Voters Driven by Fear of Losing Status, Not Economic Anxiety, Study Finds," *New York Times*, April 24, 2018, accessed July 25, 2019, https://www.nytimes.com/2018/04/24/us/politics/trump-economic-anxiety.html.

101 **Allegations of racism were a "smear":** David Maraniss, "Duke Emerges from Loss Stronger Than Ever," *Washington Post*, October 8, 1990, https://www.washingtonpost.com/archive/politics/1990/10/08/duke-emerges-from-loss-stronger-than-ever/b434133e-db6d-40b5-b6e5-55153678a4cd/.

101 **"Let them call you racists":** Eli Watkins and James Gray, "Bannon: 'Let Them Call You Racists,'" *CNN Politics*, March 11, 2018, accessed July 25,

2019, https://edition.cnn.com/2018/03/10/politics/steve-bannon-national
-front/index.html.

102   **aimed at those only with an "IQ over 120":** Southern Poverty Law Center (SPLC) Extremist Files, s.v. "Greg Johnson," accessed October 30, 2020, https://www.splcenter.org/fighting-hate/extremist-files/individual/greg-johnson.

102   **"epicenter of 'academic' white nationalism":** SPLC Extremist Files, s.v. "Greg Johnson."

103   **"I think that whites are superior to some groups":** SPLC Extremist Files, s.v. "Greg Johnson."

104   **"Never before has the black race of Central Africa":** *Encyclopaedia Britannica*, s.v. "John C. Calhoun," last updated January 13, 2021, accessed October 30, 2020, https://www.britannica.com/biography/John-C-Calhoun.

108   **"Democrats—the longer they talk about identity politics, I got 'em":** Steve Bannon, quoted in Robert Kuttner, "How Democrats Can Make Race a Winning Issue," *American Prospect*, September 4, 2018, https://prospect.org/article/how-democrats-can-make-race-winning-issue.

108   **"pale, stale males":** Simon Jenkins, "Pale, Stale Males Are the Last Group It's OK to Vilify," *Guardian*, December 15, 2016, accessed July 25, 2019, https://www.theguardian.com/commentisfree/2016/dec/15/pale-stale-males-blamed-brexit-trump.

108   **"like what it must have been like to be a black person":** Karl McDonald, "Sir Simon Jenkins: I Feel Like a Black Person Must Have 30 Years Ago," *Independent*, December 16, 2016, accessed July 25, 2019, https://inews.co.uk/inews-lifestyle/people/sir-simon-jenkins-i-feel-like-black-person-must-30-years-ago/.

109   **"have whipped up racial antagonism":** Lionel Shriver, "Identity Politics Are—by Definition—Racist," *Spectator*, August 18, 2018, accessed July 25, 2019, https://www.spectator.co.uk/2018/08/identity-politics-are-by-definition-racist/.

111   **"Calamity Thesis":** Adam Serwer, "The Nationalist's Delusion," *Atlantic*, November 20, 2017, accessed July 25, 2019, https://www.theatlantic.com/politics/archive/2017/11/the-nationalists-delusion/546356/.

111   **"possessive investment in whiteness":** George Lipsitz, *The Possessive Investment in Whiteness: How White People Profit from Identity Politics*, revised and expanded edition (Philadelphia: Temple University Press, 2006), vii.

113   **Minneapolis police used force against black people:** Richard A. Oppel Jr. and Lazaro Gamio, "Minneapolis Police Use Force Against Black People at 7

Times the Rate of Whites," *New York Times*, June 3, 2020, accessed October 30, 2020, https://www.nytimes.com/interactive/2020/06/03/us/minneapolis -police-use-of-force.html.

113 **academic John McWhorter called the view:** John McWhorter, "Police Kill Too Many People—White and Black," *Time*, July 14, 2016, accessed October 30, 2020, https://time.com/4404987/police-violence/.

114 **"THUGS":** Donald Trump (@realdonaldtrump), "....These THUGS are dishonoring the memory of George Floyd, and I won't let that happen. Just spoke to Governor Tim Walz and told him that the Military is with him all the way. Any difficulty and we will assume control but, when the looting starts, the shooting starts. Thank you!" Twitter, May 29, 2020, 12:53 a.m., accessed October 30, 2020, https://twitter.com/realdonaldtrump/status/1266231100780744704.

115 **"cult of ethnicity and its zealots":** C. Vann Woodward, "Equal but Separate," *New Republic*, July 15–22, 1991, 42–43.

116 **"in the eyes of the identity politics critic":** Jonathan Dean, "Who's Afraid of Identity Politics?" LSE blog, December 9, 2016, accessed July 26, 2019, https://blogs.lse.ac.uk/politicsandpolicy/whos-afraid-of-identity-politics/.

118 **"In the atmosphere of willful indifference":** Janet Reitman, "US Law Enforcement Failed to See the Threat of White Nationalism. Now They Don't Know How to Stop It," *New York Times*, November 3, 2018, accessed July 25, 2019, https://www.nytimes.com/2018/11/03/magazine/FBI-charlottesville -white-nationalism-far-right.html.

118 **"There is simply no electoral benefit":** Sean McElwee, "If Liberals Don't Embrace Identity Politics, They Will Lose," *Outline*, January 17, 2018, accessed July 25, 2019, https:// theoutline.com/post/2953/if-liberals-dont-embrace-identity-politics-they-will-lose?zd=1&zi=6ioipdib.

CHAPTER FIVE

122 **"Americans' sketchy understanding":** Nancy Isenberg, *White Trash: The 400-Year Untold History of Class in America* (London: Atlantic Books, 2017), 13.

124 **"In order to save the forty million":** Pankaj Mishra, "How Colonial Violence Came Home: The Ugly Truth of the First World War," *Guardian*, November 10, 2017, https://www.theguardian.com/news/2017/nov/10/how-colonial -violence-came-home-the-ugly-truth-of-the-first-world-war.

125 **those who were brought over from Africa:** Tom Dart, "Textbook Passage Referring to Slaves as 'Workers' Prompts Outcry," *Guardian*, October 6, 2015,

accessed October 30, 2020, https://www.theguardian.com/education/2015/oct/05/mcgraw-hill-textbook-slaves-workers-texas.

126 **"Reject a book that says":** Fred Arthur Bailey, "Mildred Lewis Rutherford and the Patrician Cult of the Old South," *Georgia Historical Quarterly* 78, no. 3 (Fall 1994): 533.

127 **Dunning wrote that:** Tommy Song, "William Archibald Dunning: Father of Historiographic Racism Columbia's Legacy of Academic Jim Crow," Columbia University and Slavery, accessed October 30, 2020, https://columbiaandslavery.columbia.edu/content/william-archibald-dunning-father-historiographic-racism-columbias-legacy-academic-jim-crow.

127 **In a 2019 survey of high school history books:** Joe Heim, "Teaching America's Truth," *Washington Post*, August 28, 2019, accessed October 30, 2020. https://www.washingtonpost.com/education/2019/08/28/teaching-slavery-schools/?arc404=true.

128 **Teaching Tolerance project discovered:** Southern Poverty Law Center, "SPLC Report: US Education on American Slavery Sorely Lacking," news release, January 31, 2018, accessed October 30, 2018, https://www.splcenter.org/news/2018/01/31/splc-report-us-education-american-slavery-sorely-lacking.

134 **In the paper "Who Supports the Troops?":** Thomas D. Beamish, Harvey Molotch, and Richard Flacks, "Who Supports the Troops? Vietnam, the Gulf War, and the Making of Collective Memory," *Social Problems* 42, no. 3 (August 1995): 345.

136 **"rags to riches dream of a millionaire's blank check":** Thomas A. Bailey, *Essays Diplomatic and Undiplomatic of Thomas A. Bailey*, ed. Alexander Deconde and Armin H. Rappaport (New York: Appleton-Century-Crofts, 1969), 2.

138 **"actually a disguised chemical weapons factory":** Nathan J. Robinson, "Bill Clinton's Act of Terrorism," *Jacobin*, October 2016, accessed July 23, 2019, https://www.jacobinmag.com/2016/10/bill-clinton-al-shifa-sudan-bombing-khartoum/.

139 **"We are writing you because":** Muhammad Sahimi, "The Push for War with Iran," *Frontline*, PBS, October 27, 2011, accessed July 23, 2019, https://www.pbs.org/wgbh/pages/frontline/tehranbureau/2011/10/analysis-the-push-for-war-with-iran.html.

140 **"Like their confrères in 1991":** Tom Engelhardt, "In the Heart of a Dying Empire," *Salon*, September 30, 2018, accessed July 25, 2019, https://www.salon.com/2018/09/30/in-the-heart-of-a-dying-empire_partner/.

141 **"widely held to provide the standard interpretation":** Francis T. Butts, "The Myth of Perry Miller," *American Historical Review* 87, no. 3 (June 1982): 665.

141 **"wanted a coherence with which [he] could coherently begin"**: Quoted in Abram Van Engen, "How America Became 'A City Upon a Hill,'" *Humanities* 41, no. 1 (Winter 2020), accessed January 27, 2021, https://www.neh.gov/article/how-america-became-city-upon-hill; Michael Zuckerman, "Myth and Method: The Current Crises in American Historical Writing," *History Teacher* 17, no. 2 (February 1984): 224.

141 **"made whole colonies disappear"**: Zuckerman, "Myth and Method," 224.

142 **he has called Islam**: Raya Jalabi, "A History of the Bill Maher's 'Not Bigoted' Remarks on Islam," *Guardian*, October 7, 2014, accessed January 27, 2021, https://www.theguardian.com/tv-and-radio/tvandradioblog/2014/oct/06/bill-maher-islam-ben-affleck.

146 **"clear merits of eliminating Iraq's Ba'athist dictatorship"**: John Bolton, "Overthrowing Saddam Hussein Was the Right Move for the US and Its Allies," *Guardian*, February 20, 2013, accessed October 30, 2020, https://www.theguardian.com/commentisfree/2013/feb/26/iraq-war-was-justified.

147 **Gary Shapiro wrote in 2017**: Gary Shapiro, "The Meaning of Our Confederate 'Monuments,'" *New York Times*, May 15, 2017, accessed October 30, 2020, https://www.nytimes.com/2017/05/15/opinion/the-meaning-of-our-confederate-monuments.html.

149 **"I think the right thing is to acknowledge"**: Sanjoy Majumder, "David Cameron Marks British 1919 Amritsar Massacre," *BBC News*, February 20, 2013, accessed July 25, 2019, https://www.bbc.co.uk/news/uk-politics-21515360.

149 **argues Rajiv Joseph**: Stuart Jeffries, "Visions of India: How Film and TV Romanticises Life After the Raj," *Guardian*, June 17, 2017, accessed October 30, 2020, https://www.theguardian.com/film/2017/jun/17/how-film-and-tv-romanticises-life-in-india-after-the-raj.

CHAPTER SIX

150 **"Revolutionary men with principles"**: Nawal El Saadawi, *Woman at Point Zero* (London: Zed Books, 2015), 119.

154 **"pursuit of happiness is a pointless goal"**: Tim Lott and Jordan Peterson, "The Pursuit of Happiness Is a Pointless Goal," *Observer*, January 21, 2018, accessed July 22, 2019, https://www.theguardian.com/global/2018/jan/21/jordan-peterson-self-help-author-12-steps-interview.

155 **"what was decided among the prehistoric Protozoa"**: Patrick Geddes and J. Arthur Thomson, *The Evolution of Sex* (London: Walter Scott, 1889), 267.

156 **anatomy of the corpus callosum:** Jennifer Robertson, ed., *Same-Sex Cultures and Sexualities: An Anthropological Reader* (Oxford: Blackwell Publishing, 2005), 34.

156 **"female brain is predominantly hardwired for empathy":** Simon Baron-Cohen, *The Essential Difference: The Truth About the Male and Female Brain* (New York: Basic Books, 2003), 1.

157 **"Men and Women Really Do Think Differently, Say Scientists":** Mark Bridge and Tom Whipple, "Men and Women Really Do Think Differently, Say Scientists," *Times* (London), November 13, 2018, accessed July 22, 2019, https://www.thetimes.co.uk/article/men-and-women-do-think-differently -say-scientists-sex-differences-bbfkhgs3h.

157 **The *New Statesman* published a closer inspection:** Gina Rippon, "No, That Study Doesn't Prove That Men and Women Think Differently," *New Statesman*, November 20, 2018, accessed July 22, 2019, https:// www.newstatesman.com/politics/feminism/2018/11/no-study-doesn-t-prove -men-and-women-think-differently.

158 **"The problem with men":** *Newsnight*, BBC Two, November 1, 2017.

158 **"The rules are being redrawn":** Douglas Murray, "Blurred Lines," *Spectator*, November 4, 2017, accessed July 22, 2019, https://www.spectator.co.uk/2017/11/ the-consequence-of-this-new-sexual-counter-revolution-no-sex-at-all/.

158 **journalist Peter Hitchens went down the creative route:** Peter Hitchens, "What Will Women Gain from All This Squawking about Sex Pests? A Niqab," *Mail on Sunday*, November 5, 2017, accessed 22 July, 2019, https:// www.dailymail.co.uk/debate/article-5050887/What-women-gain-squawking -sex-pests-Niqab.html.

158 **ironically resigned confusion:** Giles Coren, "A Couple of XX's Could End My Glorious Career," *Times* (London), October 21, 2017, accessed July 22, 2019, https://www.thetimes.co.uk/article/a-couple-of-misplaced-kisses-co uld-end-my-career-plwzh6n3l.

159 **wondered if women are just hardwired:** Rod Liddle, "It's Not Victim Blam-ing to Suggest There Might Be Two Sides to Every Story," *Spectator*, Novem-ber 4, 2017, accessed July 22, 2019, https://www.spectator.co.uk/2017/11/its -not-victim-shaming-to-suggest-there-might-be-two-sides-to-every-story/.

159 **#MeToo a "sexual inquisition":** Brendan O'Neill, "Who Will Put a Brake on This Sexual Inquisition?" *Spiked*, November 6, 2017, accessed July 22, 2019, https://www.spiked-online.com/2017/11/06/who-will-put-a-brake-on-this -sexual-inquisition/.

159 **Michael White went on BBC radio:** Rachel Wearmouth, "Ex-*Guardian* Columnist Calls Female Political Journalists 'Predators' Who Trick 'Poor Old Ugly' MPs," *Huffington Post*, November 2, 2017, accessed July 22, 2019, https://www.huffingtonpost.co.uk/entry/guardian-michael-white_uk_59fa015be4b00c6145e353fc.

159 **nuance between rape and other forms of sexual assault:** Bret Stephens, "When #MeToo Goes Too Far," *New York Times*, December 20, 2017, accessed July 22, 2019, https://www.nytimes.com/2017/12/20/opinion/metoo-damon-too-far.html.

160 **sexism in the UK is more "in your face":** "UN Special Rapporteur Rashida Manjoo Says UK Has 'Sexist Culture'" *BBC News*, April 15, 2014, accessed July 22, 2019, https://www.bbc.co.uk/news/uk-27034117.

160 **rapes in London rose by 20 percent:** Lizzie Dearden, "London Sees 20% Rise in Rape Reports in a Year, but Police Admit They 'Don't Understand' Reason," *Independent*, February 23, 2018, accessed July 22, 2019, https://www.independent.co.uk/news/uk/crime/rape-london-reports-met-police-rise-crime-sexual-assault-a8225821.html.

162 **three women a day are killed:** "Violence Against Women in the United States: Statistics," National Organization for Women, accessed July 23, 2019, https://now.org/resource/violence-against-women-in-the-united-states-statistic/.

162 **hovering around 38 percent:** "Violence Against Women," World Health Organization, November 29, 2017, accessed July 23, 2019, https://www.who.int/news-room/fact-sheets/detail/violence-against-women.

162 **In England and Wales:** *Telegraph* Reporters, "900 Women Have Been Killed by Men in England and Wales over the Past 6 Years," *Telegraph*, December 7, 2016, accessed July 23, 2019, https://www.telegraph.co.uk/women/life/900-women-have-killed-men-england-wales-past-6-years/.

164 **twenty-seven abortion bans were enacted:** Elizabeth Nash, "Unprecedented Wave of Abortion Bans Is an Urgent Call to Action," Guttmacher Institute, May 22, 2018, accessed July 23, 2019, https://www.guttmacher.org/article/2019/05/unprecedented-wave-abortion-bans-urgent-call-action.

164 **there was a similar slowing down of positive trends:** *The Global Gender Gap Report 2017* (Geneva: World Economic Forum, 2017), accessed July 23, 2019, http://www3.weforum.org/docs/WEF_GGGR_2017.pdf.

165 **"None of us will see gender parity in our lifetimes":** "Mind the 100 Year Gap," World Economic Forum, December 16, 2019, accessed October 30,

2020, https://www.weforum.org/reports/gender-gap-2020-report-100-years
-pay-equality.

166 **In 2018, a Sky poll on the question:** Harry Carr, "Feminism Has Gone
Far Enough, Most Britons Say," *Sky News*, March 7, 2018, accessed October
30, 2020, https://news.sky.com/story/feminism-has-gone-far-enough-most
-britons-say-11278752.

166 **In a 1994 PBS episode of *Think Tank*:** "Has Feminism Gone Too Far?" *Think
Tank*, PBS, transcript, November 4, 1994, accessed July 23, 2019, https://
www.pbs.org/thinktank/transcript132.html.

168 **"too contrived, too slick":** Marie Lindberg, "8 Quotes That Prove Republicans Haven't Learned from Anita Hill or #MeToo," People for the American
Way, September 26, 2018, accessed October 30, 2020, https://www.pfaw.org/
blog-posts/8-quotes-that-prove-republicans-havent-learned-from-anita-hill
-or-metoo/.

169 *When Men Murder Women*: *When Men Murder Women: An Analysis of 2015
Homicide Data* (Washington, DC: Violence Policy Center, September 2017),
accessed October 30, 2020, https://www.vpc.org/studies/wmmw2017.pdf.

169 **only 7 percent of cases resulted in a conviction:** Kathleen Daly and Brigitte
Bouhours, "Rape and Attrition in the Legal Process: A Comparative Analysis
of Five Countries," *Crime and Justice* 39, no. 1 (2010): 565–650, accessed July
23, 2019, https://core.ac.uk/download/pdf/143870355.pdf.

172 **2015 Birmingham University study:** Natalie Braber, "Representation of
Domestic Violence in Two British Newspapers, *The Guardian* and *The Sun*,
2009–2011," *English Language Research*, no. 1 (2014): 86–104, accessed July
23, 2019, https://www.birmingham.ac.uk/Documents/college-artslaw/elal/elr
-journal/issue-1/ELR-Braber.pdf.

173 **"redistribution of sex":** Ross Douthat, "The Redistribution of Sex," *New
York Times*, May 2, 2018, accessed July 23, 2019, https://www.nytimes.com
/2018/05/02/opinion/incels-sex-robots-redistribution.html.

173 **"previously, pleasantly, progressive":** Amy Butcher, "MIA: The Liberal Men
We Love," *Literary Hub*, February 27, 2018, accessed July 23, 2019, https://
lithub.com/mia-the-liberal-men-we-love/.

175 **"Men view even small losses of deference":** William J. Goode, "Why
Men Resist," *Dissent* (Spring 1980), accessed July 23, 2019, https://
www.dissentmagazine.org/article/why-men-resist.

177 **fathers were as likely as mothers:** Gretchen Livingston and Kim Parker,

"8 Facts about American Dads," Pew Research Center, June 12, 2019, https://www.pewresearch.org/fact-tank/2019/06/12/fathers-day-facts/.

178   **"wielding anti-feminism as a political cudgel":** Ishaan Tharoor, "How Anti-Feminism Is Shaping World Politics," *Washington Post*, January 30, 2018, accessed July 23, 2019, https://www.washingtonpost.com/news/worldviews/wp/2018/01/30/how-anti-feminism-is-shaping-world-politics/?utm_term=.599465193223.

CONCLUSION

180   **men are 3.5 times more likely to die by suicide:** Helene Schumacher, "Why More Men Than Women Die by Suicide," *BBC Future*, March 18, 2019, accessed July 25, 2019, http://www.bbc.com/future/story/20190313-why-more-men-kill-themselves-than-women.

181   **"I voted for him, and he's the one who's doing this":** Patricia Mazzei, "'It's Just Too Much': A Florida Town Grapples With a Shutdown After a Hurricane," *New York Times*, January 7, 2019, quoted in Zack Beauchamp, "'He's Not Hurting the People He Needs to Be': A Trump Voter Says the Quiet Part Out Loud," *Vox*, January 8, 2019, accessed July 25, 2019, https://www.vox.com/policy-and-politics/2019/1/8/18173678/trump-shutdown-voter-florida.

182   **"Now, who will stand against Tyranny":** Alan Feuer, "Free Speech Scholars to Alex Jones: You're Not Protected," *New York Times*, August 7, 2018, accessed October 30, 2020, https://www.nytimes.com/2018/08/07/business/media/alex-jones-free-speech-not-protected.html.

182   **"We're losing the thread":** Jacqueline Thomsen, "Bill Maher Criticizes Social Media Bans: 'Alex Jones Gets to Speak,'" *Hill*, August 18, 2018, accessed July 25, 2019, https://thehill.com/policy/technology/technology/402450-bill-maher-on-social-media-bans-alex-jones-gets-to-speak.

183   **"is to negate the implicit assurance":** Stanley Fish, "The Harm in Free Speech," *New York Times*, June 4, 2012, accessed July 25, 2019, https://opinionator.blogs.nytimes.com/2012/06/04/the-harm-in-free-speech/.

184   **"We willingly turned the other way":** Janet Reitman, "US Law Enforcement Failed to See the Threat of White Nationalism. Now They Don't Know How to Stop It," *New York Times*, November 3, 2018, accessed July 25, 2019, https://www.nytimes.com/2018/11/03/magazine/FBI-charlottesville-white-nationalism-far-right.html.

185 **"You get beat up":** Jane Coaston, "The Proud Boys, Explained," *Vox,* October 1, 2020, accessed October 30, 2020, https://www.vox.com/2018/10/15/17978358 /proud-boys-trump-biden-debate-violence.

185 **report by the Anti-Defamation League's Center on Extremism revealed:** Anti-Defamation League, "ADL Report: White Supremacist Murders More Than Doubled in 2017," news release, January 17, 2018, accessed July 25, 2019, https://www.adl.org/news/press-releases/adl-report-white-supremacist -murders-more-than-doubled-in-2017.

185 **according to the Stimson Center:** Stimson, *Stimson Study Group on Counterterrorism Spending: Protecting America While Promoting Efficiencies and Accountability* (Washington, DC: Stimson Center, 2018), 7, accessed October 30, 2020, https://www.stimson.org/wp-content/files/file-attachments /CT_Spending_Report_0.pdf.

186 **"They could look at the wealthy persons":** Sean Illing, "How the Politics of Racial Resentment Is Killing White People," *Vox,* March 19, 2019, accessed July 25, 2019, https://www.vox.com/2019/3/19/18236247/dying-of-whiteness -trump-politics-jonathan-metzl.

186 **"Mugged by Reality":** Peter Baker, " 'Mugged by Reality,' Trump Finds Denial Won't Stop the Pandemic," *New York Times,* July 24, 2020, accessed October 30, 2020, https://www.nytimes.com/2020/07/24/us/politics/coronavirus -trump-denial.html.

187 **"election of Donald Trump to the Presidency":** David Remnick, "An American Tragedy," *New Yorker,* November 9, 2016, accessed July 25, 2019, https:// www.newyorker.com/news/news-desk/an-american-tragedy-2.

191 **chief of naval operations tweeted:** Admiral Michael Gilday (@USNavyCNO), "Today, I directed my staff to begin crafting an order that would prohibit the Confederate battle flag from all public spaces and work areas aboard Navy installations, ships, aircraft and submarines," Twitter, June 9, 2020, 1:24 p.m., accessed October 30, 2020, https://twitter.com/USNavyCNO /status/1270451752459010049.

192 **The message said:** Tom Cotton, "Tom Cotton: Send In the Troops," *New York Times,* June 3, 2020, accessed October 30, 2020, https:// www.nytimes.com/2020/06/03/opinion/tom-cotton-protests-military.html.

192 **"Given the life-and-death importance of the topic":** Cotton, "Send in the Troops."

192 **"tired of shouldering the burden":** NewsGuild of Greater Philadelphia, "We

Hear Our Members of Color; Now the *Inquirer* Must," news release, (June 3, 2020, accessed October 30, 2020, https://www.local-10.com/2020/06/we-hear-our-members-of-color-now-the-inquirer-must/.

193 **A letter published by *Harper's* magazine:** Elliot Ackerman et al., "A Letter on Justice and Open Debate," letter to the editor, *Harper's*, July 7, 2020, accessed October 30, 2020, https://harpers.org/a-letter-on-justice-and-open-debate/.